# *An Amazing Woman! The Helene Hines Story*
## *Living with MS and Enjoying Life*

*Barbara M. Vitale*

Jay Street Publishers, New York, NY 10023

Published by Jay Street Publishers
155 West 72nd Street, New York, NY 10023

ISBN 0-9639999-7-4

With love, respect and admiration to Helene and her family and all the wonderful people in her MS classes.

I wish to thank my family and friends too numerous to list who encouraged me throughout the writing of this book.

**"I've run 27 marathons –
with multiple sclerosis!"**

# WHAT LIFE IS ALL ABOUT

I can hardly walk, my hands are numb,
My eyesight is the pits.
My bladder belongs to a 90-year-old.
It really tests my wits.

Sometimes I don't swallow too well.
But drooling I do a lot.
And my balance, well, it doesn't exist.
People think I'm drunk, when I'm not!

I've tried the buffet of meds
That doctors have offered to me.
Shot after shot and pill and pill,
An improvement I just don't see.

So why haven't I killed myself?
Why haven't I taken the easy way out?
Because my friends, my fellow sufferers,
That's not what life is about!

If I fall, I get up.
If I drop it, I pick it up.
If I need help, I ask.
And I'll attempt every task.

Sometimes I'm not successful.
More often I'm not.
Most times I'm awkward
But I give graceful a shot.

But I'm happy, I'm in love,
And many love me.
My life is fufilled
In that it's the best it can be.

And I'll make it better
Each year that I live
By enjoying my ability
To love and to give.

Let's all make a resolution
For 2002
That M.S. will not determine
What we can and can not do.

Let's forge forward
And improve bit by bit
By being mentally upbeat
And physically fit.

And don't ever give up!
And don't ever tune out!
Because, my friends,
That's not what life is about!

*Linda Barshak*

# TABLE OF CONTENTS

# INTRODUCTION

I first met Helene (the Maniac) Hines through a friend shortly after school opened, during my first year of retirement from teaching. By coincidence or fate my friend met Helene on the crowded boardwalk in Long Beach; Helene told her how she needed help with a Multiple Sclerosis (MS) water exercise class. And because I was no longer actively teaching, I was looking for something to do. This seemed ideal. It was in my field of physical education and close to where I lived, so I decided to volunteer.

When I arrived at the pool my first day, Helene was in the water and gestured to me to "come play with us." There were several people in the pool moving and working with foam dumbbells and noodles. In the water I couldn't tell they had MS.

The first thing I noticed of Helene was her medium long blonde hair and warm and bright blue-gray eyes. What really struck me though, was her tight athletic body. She was in better shape than an athletic 20-year-old, yet she was 52. You could not tell she had MS, even on land. When the session was over and the students left the pool, I was amazed at how hard it was for them to move on land compared to how free they were in the water. From a physical educator's point of view, I was impressed with the workout Helene had given them. However, I did not realize at the time what an extraordinary person she is. Somehow, although I didn't know it then, she was impressed with me, too.

I left feeling useful and productive again and told her I would come back. After a while, I came to help with both her classes. She had one on Monday evenings and another on Thursday mornings. After a Thursday class, Helene asked that I bike with her. She used a hand-cranked wheel chair, which I thought would be way too slow for me, but as a favor to her I went. I knew she was training to bike in the marathon. What a surprise when I had trouble keeping up with her. She never wanted to go slower than 13 m.p.h. even against the wind, and preferred 15 to 17 m.p.h.

Although she was just using her arms to do this, while I had the full force of my legs, I couldn't admit it was hard for me. My legs were burning and we hardly stopped to rest for the 16 miles we were out there. Later that day, she had boxing to improve her balance, and a water aerobics class to teach that night. That is when I nicknamed her The Maniac. After that, we biked often and she took me kayaking to cross train. Exercise was her therapy I discovered.

Bit by bit I learned about Helene Hines. She never bragged, so it came out gradually. One night, she was being given an award by the local chamber of commerce. I heard Larry Elovich, a prominent lawyer in Long Beach, refer to her as a world class athlete who ran 27 marathons. Now unable to run due to MS, she bikes these marathons in her hand-cranked wheel chair, and wins. He also told how he foolishly accepted a push-up challenge from Helene. He couldn't believe a woman could do more than him, but when he stopped at 65, she continued to 75.

Another time she was a guest speaker at an MS support group. She asked me to attend. She told me that I could give a different perspective than her on how the water therapy was helping. She wanted to recruit more people to her classes. Actually, I think I was invited, because, besides MS, Helene is also mechanically disabled and needed me to work the VCR with her video.

Watching the video and hearing her story, I began to

realize what an extraordinary women she was, and I couldn't say no to her for anything after that. When she wanted someone to bike with her, even in 20-degree winter weather, I went. When she put on a boxing demonstration for people with MS at a concert, she told me, not asked, that I was doing the sound effects for her. The more I saw of Helene, the more I was amazed and inspired by her. Also, with all the exercise I was getting, I dropped a size in my jeans. I thought I was in good shape before meeting her, but after a few months with her, I was in the best physical shape I had ever been.

I heard how MS had left her paralyzed, but rather than succumb to a wheel chair she crawled around the house. I heard how exercise helped her, and how exercise in the water was possible even for those who couldn't do it on land. Having found help for herself, she now was seeking to help others with the same illness.

This would be enough to write a book about Helene, The Maniac, Hines but there is more. Suddenly, without any symptoms, she was diagnosed with a cancerous tumor on her kidney. The kidney had to be removed, a serious operation for anyone. With MS and her fluctuating blood pressure, the operation was even more complicated. She bounced back, remarkably fast, and in 7½ weeks after the operation, entered and won first place in the women's wheel chair division of the New York City marathon. Only two men in the men's wheel chair division came in slightly ahead of her.

Two years later she underwent shoulder replacement surgery. Within three months after the procedure she entered the Boston Marathon and finished first again.

In the pages that follow' is the story of the amazing, inspirational Helene, The Maniac, Hines whose motto has been: "Place your mind on your objective, then let your body follow."

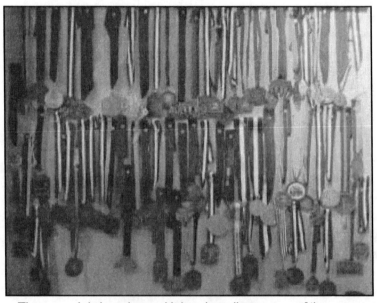

These medals hanging on Helene's wall are some of the many
awards she has earned.

# THE BEGINNING

Helene was born in New York City on January 29, 1949, the oldest of two girls. Her mother majored in journalism and her father was a mechanical engineer who holds a patent for the automatic pilot.

She grew up in Long Beach, a barrier island off the coast of Long Island surrounded by the Atlantic Ocean to the south, Reynolds Channel to the North, the towns of Lido Beach and Point Lookout to the east and Atlantic Beach to the west. Long Beach featured a two mile plus boardwalk along the shore with beautiful white sandy beaches.

Helene's childhood was typical of suburban America in the fifties. She was an active tomboy and at times a little too wild. At one point she hit other toddlers with her shovel in the sandbox, and when she came to play, other parents took their children away. For the most part though, she was well adjusted, had friends, and was a good student throughout her school years.

She attended a progressive school in New York City for a while, and then spent the rest of her school years in Long Beach. In high school she went out for every sport that was available to girls at the time, although, according to Helene, she really wasn't an exceptional athlete. She just enjoyed participating in them.

After high school, because of her interest in sports, her parents suggested she become a physical education teacher. Helene agreed, and attended Sargent College in Boston, part of Boston University.

While in college, Helene met her husband, George. One night, Helene went to the library with a grad student who was tutoring her. Helene decided to make this a "hunting" expedition. She dressed in a sexy outfit, but camouflaged herself with books, and was introduced to the others at the table. She sat next to an unsuspecting medical student, set her trap, and he was hooked. A little shy, he told her tutor that he would like to go out with her and asked him to get her number for him. On the phone they talked like what seemed forever to Helene, before he asked her out.

For their very first date they went to a gym where Helene promptly flipped him on a mat, showing off what she learned in judo class. In spite of this, or maybe because of this, George did call for a second date.

"I must have been desperate," he jokes now. George worked at the Boston Garden, being on call in case first aid was needed at the hockey games. Many of their early dates were watching the games while he was working. Helene hated hockey, but went along to be with him. After several pecks, Helene couldn't take it anymore, and attacked him with real kisses one night in the elevator from the 18th floor on down.

They married after college and had two children. George started his internship at Maimonedes in Brooklyn and then Helene followed him to Michigan where Brian was born. Helene was very unhappy there, and they returned to New York. George finished his residency in surgery at Long Island Jewish and Jennifer was born at that time. He then went to New York University for his fellowship. Those were a rough couple of years, Helene recalls, with two young children and hardly seeing her husband. She remembers him coming home with blood on his clothes and too exhausted to do anything. She even asked him to switch his field of specialization. Helene also admits to being rather bitchy at times. Once, she changed the locks on the doors, and another time brought in non-kosher food so George wouldn't eat in the house.

14

The marriage made it through all this. Helene stopped picking on George and to help make ends meet and keep her head together, Helene taught part time exercise and swimming classes at the Waterside Health Club. At that time, even with all his hard work and long hours, she earned more than he did.

Later on, Helene continued her career, teaching physical education at the Woodmere Academy on Long Island, and then in the Long Beach public schools.

The first episode of MS probably occurred while Helene was still in college, but it was not diagnosed as such. Part of the physical education curriculum was a strenuous camping course. The students were required to engage in a lot of outdoor living, including portages (the carrying of canoes and equipment over long distances). One day while this was going on, Helene's legs seemed to give out. She had trouble keeping up and couldn't pull her share of the work. The other girls, instead of being sympathetic, looked upon Helene as some spoiled brat trying to get out of the work. This made it doubly hard for Helene, who didn't know what was happening to her. At the time it was thought to be herniated disks in the back and neck and the condition cleared up. In retrospect this was probably the beginning of her bout with MS. Perhaps the over-exertion coupled with the stress of losing a grandparent had something to do with triggering it off, but no one really knows. It was very scary for Helene, but fortunately the attack did not repeat itself.

Years later, at the age of 30, Helene was suddenly unable to lift her racket while playing tennis with her husband. She didn't fall or twist anything in the swing, but something was wrong and she couldn't move her neck.

"What's wrong?" George asked, as Helene sat down on the court.

"I don't know. I just can't seem to turn my head."

"Where does it hurt?"

"It doesn't hurt. I don't know what's going on."

Playing with three doctors who thought she probably had some sort of minor neck strain, they told her to rest as they finished the game. She lay down in the back of the court, but when it was time to go, she had to hold her head in her hands to get up. At home she was given valium and the group went out to dinner, still believing it was a minor injury.

When the neck strain didn't clear up, George insisted that she see a doctor. After several tests, the doctor prescribed therapy for her neck again attributing it to herniated disks. But that, apparently was not the real cause of the problem. The therapy did not help. Instead of improving, she felt she was slowly getting worse. Helene had trouble moving about. Her legs were getting weaker and weaker. She felt she was becoming paralyzed. The numbness started low on her legs and was creeping higher. How high was it going to go?

Now a mother of two, Helene was terrified. Would she go to sleep and have the paralysis go up her chest to the point where she couldn't breathe? What will happen to her the next morning? How was she going to take care of her children? Her son, Brian, was now 8; and Jennifer was 6.

All these fears were going through her; she was no longer able to juggle the life of a wife, mother and teacher. Indeed, just getting around the house was now an overwhelming task and nobody seemed to know what was the cause of all this, let alone the cure. Her friends noticed something was very wrong with the way she moved and felt. One friend said she walked like the tin soldier in the Wizard of Oz.

George, although a doctor, must have been in denial at this time. He and the children didn't seem to notice what she was going through, which made things even more

Helen and George Hines, June 1993

difficult for Helene.

One day, she called George at work and complained, "I can't move!"

"What do you mean, you can't move?"

"What does 'I can't move' mean? George, I literally can't move!"

"Go to the doctor."

"How? I can't move." George immediately rushed home and they went to a neurologist, who put her into the hospital immediately.

"I can't believe you waited all this time before coming to me!" he exclaimed. He ordered a mylogram. Helene, meanwhile, suddenly feared she might have MS. Her aunt had it, but the doctor said no.

Expecting to find something wrong in her neck and back, she was being prepared for emergency surgery while waiting for test results. The mylogram showed nothing however, so they were stumped. Perhaps a virus. She was given steroids by I.V. while in the hospital for a week. The physical therapist arranged to treat her was on vacation, but no replacement was sent. The first neurologist got sick himself, and another was called in. After a week of anguish, Helene decided to boost her spirits by getting her hair done at the hospital salon. The doctor felt if she was well enough for this, she might as well go home. She still couldn't walk.

Her mother was interviewing maids and nurses. At home Helene was stuck upstairs, feeling helpless and frightened. She broke down and cried. George felt she should rest and didn't want anyone to bother her. Knowing how her well-meaning parents could upset her, George told the maid not to let them or anyone else visit Helene who might bother her.

When her parents rang the bell and the maid would not allow them to come in, Helene's father broke the door down to get to his baby.

After that experience, the maid quit. Helene, refusing to give in to a wheel chair, crawled around the house, struggling to be independent.

By now a third neurologist was consulted and he gave her oral steroids and told her to rest. He was also the doctor who finally diagnosed her illness as MS, and gave her the discouraging news that there was very little he could do to help her.

He advised Helene to call him each week. But as the weeks went by, she showed no improvement. Brian, who was a real little man, helped his mother when George wasn't home. George, felt helpless, even more so because he was a doctor. He watched his wife go from a strong and independent physical educator, to a weak and dependent woman. He was scared, although he didn't relay this fear to Helene. He threw his arms around her to console her. She couldn't see that his eyes were swollen with tears.

Helene somehow managed to take care of the kids, but it was very scary. She became depressed, cried, got angry and experienced all those other emotions that people go through when they are diagnosed with a serious illness. However, something inside of her said, "Don't give up," and she fought these negative feelings.

George was so good to her, Helene remembers. He was a huge help when he came home and each night they went for a "walk." Actually, Helene really couldn't walk as we define walking. George would hold her up and she forced herself to put one foot in front of the other. First, they walked to the next house, then two houses, then half the block, etc. Helene refused to let her legs atrophy. She would crawl before she used a wheel chair. Somehow, she felt once she took the easier route of a wheel chair, she would never get out of it. So she did what she could during the day, and went on her walks at night

Helene noticed a strange thing with human behavior. As she became disabled and walked strangely, people began to treat her differently than heretofore. Of course she was still the same person, but people reacted differently to her now. This was something else she had to learn to adjust to. She still notices this. People react differently when she has her canes with her than when she does not.

One night on television, Helene saw a program on paraplegics. They were using stim pads to electrically stimulate the muscles to force them to contract.

"George!" she cried out, "Come listen to this!"

The program lit a flicker of hope in Helene. She and George discussed it, and agreed that Helene should try it.

# WALK AND RUN

Helene and George found an orthopedist that had stim and regular therapy at his facility. At the consultation he listened carefully to what Helene told him.

"In your case I don't feel the stim therapy will work," he said, but not to discourage her completely, added, "but it certainly cannot hurt. So lets give it a try." He asked her what medicines she was on and what she was doing up to then. Helene had been going for physical therapy, but they used heat treatments, which he said was harming the condition.

Helene now says, "You really have to carefully choose your doctors. There I was conscientiously doing everything the other therapist advised me, and it was the wrong thing to do."

The stim therapy involved putting little pads on various parts of the muscles. Helene would lie down on a table and a low dose of electricity was sent into the muscle. The therapist was very cautious and started her on very low doses and gradually increased them. Helene felt her thigh tighten and her leg lifted up off the table. She kind of liked the feel of it, although some other people could not tolerate it.

"It felt good to feel the mush of my thigh harden for a few seconds, and feel the way it used to before the MS."

Helene went about four times a week.

One time the treatment felt a little too good. The technician had placed the pad a little too high on her thigh. Helene told him it wasn't right, but he said it was. A moment later, the first electrical shock threw Helene into an orgasm she remembers with some embarrassment. She called one of the girls over and whispered in her ear what was happening. They both laughed, the pad was moved and the machine was nicknamed, Pierre, from that moment on.

Although the treatments felt good, Helene didn't see any improvement in her condition. However, every now and then, her legs felt a little sore, sort of like a charley horse, so she knew something was happening in those muscles. She knew that if they were sore as if she just had a work out, they must be getting stronger. So she continued the treatments, and she and George went for their walks, but it was months before there was noticeable improvement.

Eventually she found she was able to walk better, and she and George would go on the boardwalk for their strolls. George liked to jog and he would do the length of the boardwalk and back, a distance of about four and a half miles. He would help Helene, go on his run, and come back for her. As Helene was able to move better and longer distances, George noticed that he wasn't holding her up as much any more. Soon she was beginning to walk a bit on her own. George would start out with her, jog his four plus miles and wherever he met her on the way back would walk home with her.

By this time the doctor had noticed an increase in Helene's leg strength and suggested therapy on the machines. Again, he started her out very slowly with gradual increases. Helene and George were both encouraged and so was the doctor. They had confidence in him and tried everything he suggested. She was put on various medications, some hard to acquire in this country, and others still experimental.

Now when Helene and George went for their walks, Helene discovered that she could jog a little. Her form wasn't good; Helene had never been a runner before. Somehow, though, it felt more comfortable to run than to walk. Helene and George would slowly trot a short distance together, then he would run by himself along the boardwalk, return, meet her and resume their slow joint trot.

As the distance Helene was running improved, she and George decided to enter one of Long Beach's short races. The community sponsors various races throughout the year, usually at different holidays. Helene and George decided to start with the shortest one, the 2K race. It gave Helene a little more motivation. There was now a set goal to work on, and it made the workouts more meaningful. When the day of the event arrived, she and George were totally excited. Here she was actually participating in a race, when only a year ago she could hardly walk.

George kept pace with his wife from the beginning to the very end; Helene, miraculously, finished the race.

"What a feeling of elation came over me as I crossed the finish line," Helene recalls. "I did it! I really did it!" she exclaimed as she and George threw their arms around each other.

Although Helene had made tremendous progress compared to the time she was crawling around the house, the path wasn't easy. Multiple sclerosis is very strange and every day can be different. One day after everything was going smoothly, her neck would stiffen up and the anguish might last several days. Another time, when she leaned forward, shooting pains like electric shocks would race down her back, something common in MS patients.

"I thought I was being stabbed and quickly turned around, but no one was there."

Or one leg might go numb and she wouldn't be able to exercise or undergo therapy for a while. By the time she was able to resume her activities, her muscles had already weakened, and she had to take additional time to rebuild them to where she had left off.

"It was like taking two steps forward, and then one step backwards, and sometimes going backwards two or three steps, before going forwards again. There were times it was just so frustrating, I would get depressed. Then George would remind me of how far I had come and I would snap out of it."

Helene also began to realize that these set backs were not permanent, and she would wait them out. "When my leg would go numb, I'd know that it might last a while, but I also knew it would clear up soon. Knowing that took away a lot of the initial fear that I had in the beginning, when I didn't know it was only temporary."

Slowly, but surely, Helene had made tremendous progress. However, it took 12 years from the time of her first stim treatment until she ran her first marathon.

She was now getting well enough to enter a 5K race. As each race was entered and completed, Helene set her goal on the next one. Like any athlete in training, she had something to really strive for and focus on. Something positive to offset the negative aspects of her condition.

Helene's life had now settled into a routine. She continued with her therapy and was teaching part time, mostly with adult education, and kept training for upcoming races. Her parents weren't very supportive through all this, although they were more than willing to provide her with medical help and nurses for her condition. They could see how much better she was, but still they felt it was not the right thing for her to do. They didn't come to cheer her on at local races or to congratulate her on her achievements. Her mother-in-law, however, did both.

Once her mother told her that she was wearing out her heart. She said it only could beat so many times, and she was wasting the beats with the strenuous runs.

"It made no sense for her to talk like that. She was an educated woman. I don't know what the real problem was," remarked Helene. They did come to one race, though, a biathlon in Long Beach. Helene had successfully completed one already, and came in fifth place for her age group. However, she did have trouble with this competition, the only one attended by her parents. The biathlon had the run first and the swim second. It would been safer to schedule the swim first, but this is the way it was programmed. During the swim, Helene experienced one of her MS attacks, where she feels her throat closing up and has trouble breathing. She managed to finish the swim doing a sidestroke and yelled for an ambulance as soon as she got out of the ocean.

As Helene kept up her running and short races, she heard of the Achilles Track Club. By now, Helene had been running for about 10 years. She joined the club in 1989. That is when she began to get serious about her running. Now when she entered races, she entered to really compete, not just be a participant. Today, a wall in her home is full of trophies, medals and other awards and certificates of recognition. Many of the races offered monetary awards as well, sometimes up to $1500. Helene never kept a penny of this. She always donated all of it to charities, usually to the Achilles Club to buy a wheel chair for someone, or to Canines Companions for Independence.

The Achilles Club was founded by Dick Traum, the first amputee to run a marathon. The club is for people with disabilities who want to run. The club now has chapters all over the world.

"All you have to do is want to," Dick encouraged her. "We'll help you with the rest."

Every Tuesday evening Helene worked out with the club. She became part of a group of people about her age with various disabilities. There were coaches to help each person according to their ability.

"It was great being part of the group. Like being part

of a family, we encouraged each other," Helene remembers.

The Achilles Club used volunteer runners to help support those who were competing in the races. Eventually, after running with the Achilles club for several months, Helene felt strong enough and offered to volunteer in the marathon. She was given a very obese woman she was to meet at the 13-mile mark and run with her the rest of the race. On the day of the event Helene awoke with an MS attack, and couldn't move her neck or turn her head.

"Oh no! George, what am I going to do? That woman is counting on me. I have to go." She tried resting a bit and tried different exercises, but nothing helped. "I'll just have to go like this."

At the race she took over from the previous volunteer. "The woman was more walking than running so I was able to keep up. At times I was walking sideways, so I could face her. I was so uncomfortable the whole way."

At one point the woman "hit the wall" – she just wanted to quit.

"Oh, no, you don't!" Helene yelled. "If I came here in this state because I didn't want to let you down, then you can't let me down either."

Then in a gentler tone, "You can do it. You know you can," and Helene offered her a candy bar. "I think I fed her all the way to the finish line. I'll never forget that experience, but she did make it."

Helene also recalls doing something really foolish that day. Among the snacks she brought, Helene had sliced a banana and had put it in her pocket. Of course, by the time she reached for a slice, she got banana mush.

"I don't know how I could have been so dumb" Now she carries nicely wrapped Power Bars.

The lady did finish her first marathon and felt great. Thanks to Dick and the Achilles Club, the marathons were now changing. Instead of just being a competition for world

Helene and George in the Maine Marathon. 1998.

class athletes, the marathons were now for everybody. Completing a marathon had become an individual challenge of the indomitable human spirit. Time was not as important as finishing, and finishing was not as important as trying your best. Just being in it and accepting the challenge of it was what counted. Those who did finish, what for some was the biggest challenge of their lives, knew they could face anything after that, and conquer it.

After that grueling experience, Dick suggested that Helene herself try the next marathon. "I don't have the stamina for that. I can't do a marathon." Helene was happy with the amount of running she was able to do.

Dick responded, "I've watched you. You are strong enough. With us training you, you can do it."

Helene thought about it and how she had gone from walking to running, and from a 2k race to a 5k, and more. She decided to train for her own marathon.

12 years had passed since Helene started on her first stim treatment.

# THE MARATHON OR BUST

When Helene decided that she indeed was going to run the Long Island marathon, she began training very hard. Dick from the Achilles Club told her that if she could run 13 miles, she should be able to finish. She had already walked the 13 miles as a volunteer. However, she took it literally, and got herself up to the 13 miles and no more.

She continued to run with the Achilles group on Tuesdays and on some Saturdays. On other Saturdays there were races and she entered them. She also continued to run on the boardwalk in Long Beach with George. She wasn't concerned about time, just increasing her distance and stamina. Bit by bit, she managed to be able to run a distance of 13 miles, from November to May when the Long Island marathon was scheduled. Of course there were days when the MS was bad she couldn't train, and then would have to build herself up again.

One thing she did notice though was that the more she exercised the better she was. If she woke up stiff or sore and forced herself to move through it, she became better than if she rested. Today, when Helene wakes up in the morning, she can't do much. She is in pain, her hands and fingers are numb, her legs are weak; she can't fully function. She forces herself to move through the pain and other problems until she feels "normal" again. If she stops moving for too long, the symptoms come back.

I found this out one day while she was talking to me about some morning television programs. I asked her why she would waste time watching them, and she told me, "It takes me about an hour before I can do anything. After I wake up, it takes my body another hour or so to wake up."

By the time May came and Helene was able to run 13 miles, she finally entered the marathon. The Achilles Club gave her a volunteer runner named Jim. The race had staggered starts and he was to meet her at the 10 minute starting point wearing a bright green hat, so she could spot him easily. He was a first class runner, so to go her pace for this race would be nothing for him.

On the day of the event, Helene was both excited and apprehensive. She ran her pace and felt O.K. in the beginning. She spotted Jim and he came up beside her. "How are you doing"?

"So far so good," Helene responded.

At the 13-mile mark Helene was still going strong, but by 18 miles or so she had had it. By now the direction of the race had changed and they were running into the wind.

"Jim was great," Helene recalls. "He did everything to keep me going. He even sang to me, anything to keep my mind off what I was feeling."

At one point Helene had to go to the bathroom.

"Go ahead," Jim said, pointing to the bushes on the side of the road.

"No way! You gotta be kidding. I'll hold it."

"Suit yourself, but there aren't any porta-potties here." Indeed, there wasn't anything there at this time. Most of the runners had already come in and all the people waiting by the side with water and words of encouragement were gone. It was like there was no marathon, just her and Jim running. About another mile or so, Helene gave in to nature's call.

"I'll be right back." She left Jim for a couple of minutes to relieve herself in the bushes. "It was really horrible. I asked myself why I was doing this. My body ached all over. There was a stitch in my side that would not leave. I felt like I was dying."

At that point Jim suggested they change the pace.

Finish Line, Maine Marathon. 1998

"Let's run a bit, and then walk a bit and you will be able to make it."

Meanwhile, George was at the finish line not knowing where Helene was or what was happening. Over 4 hours had passed into the marathon as Helene trotted slowly along, sometimes running, sometimes walking, with Jim's constant vigil at her side. Finally, 5 hours and one minute after the start of the race, Helene staggered across the finish line of the 1990 Long Island marathon. Only 100 people finished the marathon that year, and Helene was one of them. She had the best time for a women with a disability and received the World Record Disabled Marathon Athlete award from the New York Road Runners Club and the Achilles Club, but at the time she felt no exuberance at all.

"I never was so wiped out. It was like being run over by a truck. I hurt all over, my legs felt like rubber and I couldn't even feel good enough to say, 'Hey, I did it'."

George was happy to see her come in and praised her for it.

"Just get the car for me," Helene gasped. "Get the car!"

He retorted, "You just ran 26 miles, you certainly can walk to the car."

Helene was too exhausted to argue, so she walked the quarter mile or so to where the car was parked.

For days afterwards Helene couldn't recover. She was sore and numb and utterly exhausted. George commented that anyone who took five hours to do a marathon shouldn't be in it. He didn't say this to be mean or discredit her. He was proud of her accomplishment and told her so, but he really felt she had pushed her body too bard.

When Dick called Helene with congratulations, Helene didn't respond with joy. He told her she should do the New York City marathon. "This was so hard because it was your first one. You did great. Look at the award you got. The city marathon is so exciting and so much different," he encouraged.

At the time, Helene couldn't think of running a block, let alone another marathon.

However, with time her body recuperated. The thrill of having finished a marathon and the meaning of the award all began to sink in, along with all the phone calls of congratulations. Finally, she decided she would try the New York City Marathon, but this time she would train better. Obviously her 13 miles of training hadn't prepared her properly for the marathon.

She read two books on running and followed their training suggestions. She joined the Road Runners, the club that sponsors the city marathon. She ran as before, but now also ran with the Road Runners in their training sessions. She became part of a group of about 10 people that became really a close knit group as time went on.

One day during one of the training runs, Helene was wearing her Achilles shirt. Lynn, who was in charge of the group, noticed the shirt and stated that Helene shouldn't be there with them if she was disabled.

"I can do anything you can do," Helene responded. And just to prove it, when the practice was over and Lynn decided to do another mile, Helene thought out loud, "' I think I will too." So she and Lynn did an extra mile that day. Afterwards, Lynn apologized and they became friends.

"The group was great to run with. We encouraged each other and made up rhymes as we went like this one, to the tune of 'Sound Off 1, 2':

> "We ain't afraid of ole cat hill.
> We'll do it backwards just for thrill.
> Sound off 1. 2. Sound off 3. 4.
> Sound off 1. 2. 3. 4."

This time Helene was not going to do the marathon unless she could get up to 20 miles. She wasn't concerned about speed, but wanted to build up her distance bit by bit until she could do the 20 fairly easily at her own pace. By this time, George, watching his wife begin training for her second marathon, also decided to try it. Now when they ran on the boardwalk, she was the one running more than he was. If she could do it with MS, he certainly should be able to do it. So 4 to 5 days a week Helene trained and George struggled to keep up with her.

By the time November came, Helene had reached her goal of 20 miles and felt she was ready. "The day of the race was so exciting. It was contagious. All of New York seemed to come together. You could feel the electricity in the air," Helene remembers. "There were what seemed like thousands of people around, not like the Long Island marathon. There were so many runners and so many enthusiastic spectators."

When the race started, Helene was with George and the others from Road Runners with whom she had trained. "Shortly into the race, we became separated due to the amount of participants. I did meet George later at one of the water stops and we stayed together after that."

Helene felt exhilarated through out the race. "Dick was right. This marathon was very different from Long Island. People were cheering us on. It felt terrific. I can't describe the feeling. In one borough of the city they were banging pots and pans as we went by. In others they shouted and cheered. People offered water or oranges or anything to help us on. It was like we were celebrities. By the time we crossed the 59th Street Bridge the crowds were screaming. It was unbelievable."

Helene learned of a strange tradition on another bridge. As the men crossed the upper level of the Verrazano Bridge, they would urinate over the side. Because of the different start times, this tradition could be very disconcerting for those crossing the lower level at the same time.

The only quiet place in the city was the Williamsburg section where the Hassidic Jews lived. They did not like the runners dressed in shorts disrupting their neighborhood, but they didn't do anything to interfere. "They just watched us in silence to let us know they disapproved."

Helene had trained properly for this event. By the time she reached the 20-mile mark she still felt strong. George told her that he wasn't feeling well. He didn't want to hold her back and told her to go on without him. "I'll see you at the finish line. You are doing great. Keep it up."

So Helene continued on, filled with the excitement and enthusiasm in the air. She easily crossed the finish line in 4 hours and 37 minutes. "This time I was thrilled. For most of the race I was right in with the heart of the crowd. I felt ecstatic emotionally, and physically. What a difference from last time." Now Helene was hooked.

"I told you so," congratulated Dick. And she immediately planned to run the next marathon, wherever it was to be held. She got another award, also from Road Runners and Achilles. This one was for the Outstanding Performance Award-Female. And so began the long list of awards that Helene was to earn in the coming years.

George finished that New York marathon, about 45 minutes after Helene, but began throwing up and couldn't enjoy his accomplishment of finishing his first marathon. Actually, he had frequently retched during the marathon.

Later that night, when he thought he had regained his normal good health, the couple celebrated the marathon at a restaurant. While waiting to be seated, Helene noticed something wrong with George. His head tilted and he started to fall down. She quickly held on to him, grabbed a chair and forced him into it as he was passing out.

She yelled for someone to call 911, and the maitre'd hearing the commotion, immediately rushed over to them. "Is something wrong with the food?"

George was treated for dehydration and was soon O.K.

# BOSTON AND MORE

The next marathon, in 1991, was scheduled for Boston. Helene continued to train for it. She met another lady from Long Beach, Linda, who was also interested in the Boston marathon, and they ran together.

George went with Helene to Boston, but did not run this one with her, although in spite of his experience after his first marathon he did run in several of them. They took their two stuffed animals with them. One was a cabbage patch doll and another a teddy bear. For some reason Helene doesn't remember when it started, these animals came on all their trips. If the marathon race was in view from the hotel window, Helene would prop them up so they could "watch" the race.

Helene's son, Brian, was now in college at Boston, studying medicine like his father. He also was going to do the marathon. She had him train until he could do 20 miles. However, at the time of the marathon, he was recovering from a stress fracture in his leg. There was some question as to whether he should run or not. The doctor had given him clearance to do so, but Helene was a little concerned. Brian, assuring his mother that he was all right, teased her; "You call that running. No matter what happens, I can crawl faster than you can run the marathon." Definitely not the thing to say to Helene.

On the day of the marathon Helene had two volunteers from the Achilles club, Cyril and Jack. They stayed with her and she needed their support. The Boston marathon was hilly and Helene wasn't fully prepared for the hills. Jack had a daughter in the area and she met them near the 20-mile mark with defizzled coke and aspirin.

Helene receiving one of her many awards.

"Whether it really helped or not, I don't know," Helene said thoughtfully. "A lot is in your mindset. If you think it helps, it probably will. Everybody has their own formula."

At the 16-mile mark they approached a big long hill. Cyril and Charles grabbed her hands and the three of them kept moving on the hill. "This is heartbreak hill. Once you get past this, you're OK," they encouraged. This made the hill a little easier to bear. Actually they lied, because shortly after that there was another hill and another, but Helene trudged on.

About the 20-mile mark, Helene saw her son, Brian, in front of her, running with a few of his fraternity brothers. "I could tell by the way he was running, that he was in trouble."

When she approached him, he looked at her painfully and said, "I'm hurting."

She answered, "Everybody hurts around this point."

"No, Ma, I'm really in trouble here." Brian was having

problems with his leg. Cyril gave him some herbal ointment to use.

"Let's get going," Jack urged. There was nothing seriously wrong with Brian, so Helene left him.

"I can't believe you're leaving me like this," he cried.

"After that comment you made to me. . ." Helene called back to him, but didn't finish the sentence.

At about three hours into the race the skies opened up and it poured. Still, Helene like the energizer battery commercial, kept right on going and going. She finished that marathon in her best time, 4 hours and 15 minutes – her best time of any marathon before or after.

Brian also finished, but in over 5 hours. His side of the story is that while he was resting on the ground his mother stepped on him and continued on.

"That is absolutely not true," Helene emphatically states. "I would never step on my son. 1 even gave him a kiss before I took off and I have witnesses to prove my side of the story. He wasn't even down. He was just trying to save face, because not only did I finish ahead of him, but I made him eat his words. I really rubbed it in. I went to the fraternity house and in front of his frat brothers 1 yelled out, 'Mommy won! Mommy won!' He had to say something."

Now Helene needed another challenge, and the New York City Ultra race was tempting her. This race is 37 miles in Central Park. She kept on with her running and training and decided to go for it. George thought she was nuts, especially on the day of the race, when it was cold and rainy. The weather was so bad, he didn't come out, although he was very supportive for every other race.

Helene had a group of volunteers that took turns running laps with her in the rain. One friend, Pete, nicknamed Pasta Pete stayed with her for 22 miles and then the others took turns so she was never alone. The weather got worse and at one point, "we were running through slush." One friend met her with warm pita bread and that "tasted soooo good."

With strong determination and one friend after another encouraging her, she did make it to the finish line. "I had hoped George would be there with warm dry clothes," she said, "but I can't really blame him."

90 people attempted the Ultra that cold December day, but only 9 finished it. Helene was one of the 9.

"I don't remember what my time was, or in what place I finished, but I wasn't last". Actually, Helene finished 7th out of the 9 with a time of 8 hours and 8 minutes.

From the Ultra race of 37 miles Helene decided to attempt the 100k (62.14 miles) race in February, just a couple of months later. Dick had suggested the Comrades Race in South Africa to her. Helene was now athletic director of the Achilles Club and knew about the Comrades Race, but had never actually thought of doing it herself. When Dick put the idea in her head, Helene decided to try 50 miles of the race in Central Park to see if she could possibly be ready for the Comrades race of 56 miles. This race, for some reason, was run in laps the opposite direction of the Ultra. Most of the regular runners went the other way for their workouts, and this could cause problems. "It is like going the wrong way on a one way street at times."

Helene trained with a young girl she had met in one of the marathons. Somewhere during the race, the girl decided to stop. There was plenty of help available and at the rest stop the girl asked for a massage. Helene queried, 'Hey what about me? I want one too."

They asked the young lady why would she need one. She had a wooden leg.

"My leg had gotten so stiff and hard that it felt like

wood. I did get a massage, but it didn't really help."

But Helene finished this race. Dick met her in his station wagon and they went out for a pizza party.

"By then I knew I was ready for Comrades."

# COMRADES AND CLINTON

The Comrades Race in South Africa began as an unltramarathon to honor the South African soldiers killed in World War I. It is probably one of the biggest races in the sportsworld. The race is unique in that near the end of the run it is acceptable practice for the runners in trouble to get help. People can actually come out and pull their "comrades" to the finish line.

When Helene told George she wanted to try the Comrades Race in South Africa, he became very upset. "Enough is enough. Are you out of your mind? This is just too much. You are not going to do it."

He was very angry and emphatic. Helene had never seen him like this. He was so supportive of everything she tried. To avoid a fight just before bedtime Helene didn't answer him. She lay awake on the bed for a long time, wondering how to deal with this.

The next morning, before she could approach George, he turned to her. "I have no right to tell you what you can and can't do. If this is what you really want, then I'll have to support you, no matter how I feel."

Helene hugged him and replied, "Thank you! I really want to try this. It means a lot to me and I want and need your support."

The press had picked up on Helene, the first person with a disability to try to run the Comrades. This race of 56 miles was for the world's top athletes. In order to enter the race participants had to run a qualifying time of 4½ hours for 26 miles, which Helene had already accomplished. During the actual race, after 4½ hours, anyone not beyond the 26-mile mark, the distance of a marathon, was eliminated. A loud horn would go off and those runners were taken off the course. The same thing happened after 11 hours to anyone still in the race who had not crossed the finish line. It was as if they never entered the race.

The press followed her like it does a celebrity from America before the race – from her stop in London to South Africa to the day of the race, during the race and afterwards. She arrived a few days before the marathon, but remained in South Africa for about two weeks. For the race she was put up in a special hotel just for the runners. George couldn't stay with her there.

Because of her MS and the reaction she might have running in the heat, the Comrades Marathon Association gave her a special dispensation. A separate start was set up for her at one o'clock in the morning. The race was due to start at 6 a.m. Dick told her there would be a team of volunteers for her, but somehow she was by herself. However, there were volunteers from South Africa who offered to stay with her. Two ran with her the first six hours.

After that, a young man stayed with her the rest of the way. "'He was so nice and offered to carry my fanny pack that I was running with. He also told me not to call it that, as fanny had a different connotation there. It referred to the private parts of a woman. He was great and stayed with me till the end of the race. He must have been pushing himself really hard because during one of the interviews after the race he collapsed and had to be taken to the medical tent. When I got home, I spotted a box of Fanny Farmer candies and sent it to him as a gift."

At the start of the race, there was an escort car and everything was set up just as it would be for any race, except that it was just for Helene, the only runner to start at 1 o'clock. With the world watching her, Helene took off at

Jogging with President Bill Clinton

After the jog, Helene is standing with President Clinton
and Dick Traum, president of the Achilles Club.

her usual marathon pace in the black of night. The race went through all sort of interesting cities.

"They really shielded me from seeing the poverty in the outer areas. What I saw was fascinating and beautiful. What a feeling to be jogging through Zulu land."

By 6 o'clock, the other runners had started. George was picked up in the elite car with champagne and caviar for the ceremonies at the start of the race. He was escorted to Helene around 10. She could only see him for a few minutes and then continued on. By 10 a.m. some of the faster runners had caught up to her, and she was in the front of the race, with all the spectators and cameras.

"It was a false sense of being in the lead, but it felt great."

She had finished the 26-mile mark in the allotted time of 4½ hours. Reporters came to question her throughout the run, and all this was being televised. Helene did finish the race in just under 12 hours; 11 hours, 59 minutes and 18 seconds to be exact and was swarmed by the press. The official end of the race wasn't until 5 o'clock when the awards would be given out. Helene had to stay awake until then, and was utterly exhausted. She hadn't slept much because of the excitement and all the press conferences. She had been up since 12 midnight to get ready for the 1 a.m. start. Then she ran 56 miles, and now just wanted to collapse.

By the time the award ceremony started, she was numb, but also exhilarated. She had finished the Comrades Race in 1994 and she was a worldwide celebrity. There she earned another award – Record for Ultra Marathon-Disabled.

When she returned to the United States, President Clinton honored her. He invited her to run with him in celebration of Americans with Disabilities Day, and of course there was more press coverage for Helene.

Dick called her and said that the President contacted

others. On the day of the run she was to meet President Clinton in Haynes Park. The secret service men told the guests not to approach him, but to wait until he came over. He walked towards them and shook hands. Helene had an Achilles shirt for him and he took his own off to put on the shirt she gave him. He said that his allergies were bothering him so he would keep it slow, about a 10-minute mile.

During the run though, he began to pick up the pace and Helene had trouble keeping up.

"Hey, wait for me! Don't leave me back here!"

The president at that point reached down and grabbed her hand to pull her along and the television cameras caught the action. The scene was on most of the local news programs in New York.

After the run, they were invited back to the Rose Room of the White House, where they chatted and were served refreshments.

"It was a wonderful experience," Helene recalled, "and he was even better looking in person and awfully nice. It really was an honor to be invited to run with him."

Helene crossing the finish line at Comrades Marathon
with volunteer. 1993.

# AHEAD OF THE GAME

Helene tried to run three marathons a year. She did the New York City marathon, Maine and Boston whenever she could.

There were periods when she couldn't run for one reason or another. One time, she had a lot of pain in one foot. It hurt to walk, let alone run. Nothing seemed to be helping and it bothered her not to keep up with her running. She found a local doctor trying some new experimental machine.

"I don't know the name of it. I think it had something to do with magnetic fields. You sat under it and did nothing for twenty minutes. It was strange. The whole room was full of people sitting quietly under these machines doing nothing."

Two weeks later, her foot was fine. The machine never was approved in this country, but Helene is sure it was what helped her. She began to run again, and entered the next marathon.

During those times when she could not run at all, she found water therapy to be a lifesaver. In the water there was freedom and it was possible to get as good a workout as on land. "I was able to exercise all my muscles to keep them from atrophying," she explained. "Just moving in the cool water was wonderful for me. It gave me a chance to keep moving when I couldn't run."

Helene has to keep moving in order to function properly. Sort of like a car with a bad battery. Once you jump-start the car, it runs fine, but once the car stops, it won't start again.

For the most part it looked as if the MS was under control. She kept working part time, did therapy, worked

44

Helene with volunteers "hugging" her to hold her head up.
1994 New York City Marathon.

out, and kept up with her running. One magazine article quoted her as saying, "When I run, no matter how hard it is or how much pain I might be in, if I can do it, I feel like I'm in control of the disease, not that it is controlling me."

She had some rough periods though, when, for example, her esophagus closed up. "That was so scary. I could hardly swallow. I was on baby foods for some time until it cleared up. It was unpleasant having to eat baby food, but it was the fear that was the worst part."

She developed asthma and would get attacks periodically. "I never knew what would trigger an attack, so I couldn't do anything to prevent it. I began to get nervous going places alone."

Helene at that time bought a cell phone that she took everywhere she went. "With the phone I felt more secure. I didn't want to drag people with me every time I went somewhere, and I didn't want to give up my lifestyle either. So I took the phone."

During one of the Boston marathons, her volunteer felt sick and couldn't finish with her. Helene was looking around for someone to buddy up with rather than run alone. She spotted a young man whom she could tell was really having trouble by the way he was struggling with each step. She went over to him, and worked him through "the wall" and they stayed together. Towards the end of the race, Helene had one of her asthma attacks and he stayed with her. "Now is my chance to help you."

Looking back at that moment, Helene says that "it probably was really stupid of me to keep going on to finish the marathon, wheezing and gasping for breath, but I just didn't want to quit."

On Helene's second New York City marathon, in 1992, she hurt her ankle. At about the 14th mile, with George throwing up every few minutes, Helene's foot gave out. Her volunteers helped her to the medical tent where she got ice for it. They told her, "We'll drive you to a Hospital."

Helene answered, "No you won't. I'm going to finish this marathon."

"You can't go on like that. It might be broken."

"Yes I can." And so the conversation went. Helene insisted on continuing, and so the volunteers had to stay with her. Helene stopped at every medical tent and got ice for her ankle. She managed to finish the marathon tied with her best time of 4 hours and 15 minutes. At the finish, George was too sick to help her, and "unless you are down and out they don't call an ambulance." So Helene went home and when she did get to the doctor the next day, she was diagnosed with a fractured ankle and put in a cast.

In 1994, at the New York City marathon, Helene had an MS attack and couldn't turn her neck or move her head, which was drooping. Her volunteers actually ran with their arms around her, holding her head up until the end. "The picture that was taken looks like everybody is hugging me, but what they were doing was keeping my head up so I could run."

She did have to drop out of one race, although it wasn't her choice. She wasn't feeling right and when they took her blood pressure, it was way too high. With MS, blood pressure would often fluctuate from high to low to normal. It was hard to regulate because it wasn't just a steady high or low. Her volunteers made her leave the race, otherwise she would have continued. In fact, Helene gave them a lot of opposition about dropping out, but they finally won. "They literally forced me to stop. They over powered me or else I would have continued."

Other people may be able to stop when they hurt or feel sick, and not think anything of it, but it is different with Helene. Helene is a competitive athlete. When athletes are in a game, they give their all and more, 110%.

When you watch a competitive sport, you would think it is a matter of life or death. When the competitor is in the game, he/she is totally focused on the event, and for those moments while the ball is in play, there is no other world. They will jump and dive and take risks that they ordinarily would not do outside of the game.

I view Helene and MS as a serious competition, with Helene at one end of the field and MS at the other, only this really is a matter of life and death. Every time Helene finishes a marathon, or receives an award, she has scored another goal and is ahead of the game. If she quits, it is a point for the invisible opponent.

People admire Helene's drive and energy and are inspired by her. In turn, she is inspired by some of the people who are in the Achilles Club. "There I see people with disabilities so much worse than mine. I also see how strong they are and all that they can manage to accomplish."

When Helene talks at various support groups, she shows slides of some of these Achilles members finishing races. "There is no excuse," she tells her listeners. "If they can do it with all their problems, so can you."

Numerous magazines have written articles on Helene and how she was beating her illness. Helene had her life in order, and now felt she wanted to help others. "When I realized how much the exercise was helping me, and how anyone could exercise in the water, I wanted to put the two together for others with MS."

She talked to the manager of Hollywood Sports, a local gym that had a pool. At no cost to the owner of the club, she wanted to have people with MS who weren't gym members be able to come to her class. There was some convincing and some red tape to get through. The class was permitted to be given as therapy. People came with doctor's notes and a therapist had to be present at the pool for each class. However, it was Helene who ran the class

George, Helene, Brien and Jennifer at Brian's wedding. 2001.

while the therapist sat there.

"It was great. People got in the water and found freedom. They could feel 'normal' in a way they could no longer do on land." Helene gave them a lot of work for balance as well as some strength training and a general aerobic workout. The class was held twice a week and continued for a year and a half. It also gave Helene a chance to continue her exercising in the water.

Unfortunately, the class had to be discontinued. Some members complained about "being in the water with cripples." Some were ignorant and worried about catching the disease; others were just uncomfortable. Helene tried to arrange classes at the City of Long Beach's recreation center pool. The city manager actually asked her if MS was contagious in the water. But because the pool had steps to the entrance that would make it impossible for people to access with walkers and wheel chairs, classes could not be held there. Sadly, Helene had to cease her teaching project.

Fortunately, she was able to teach an adult-education class at the Long Beach High School pool, so she managed to continue her own aqua therapy there. However, it really bothered her that she had to stop the MS aqua class after she saw how well it worked. This pool was also not accessible for wheel chairs or walkers. A few of the people who had been enrolled in the MS class, and were physically able to, attended the adult education class. But the others, who needed it the most, were unable to make it.

After a while Helene did get a call to hold an MS water class in Plainview, Long Island. "The people there just wanted to socialize and walk around in the water. They weren't receptive to the workouts I wanted to give them. It was just so frustrating, so I stopped doing the class."

Although water-therapy is very common today for all kind of ailments, Helene was probably one of the originators of this movement.

# THE FIRE DEPARTMENT

Shortly after Helene was diagnosed with MS, she was sitting on the beach with two other friends. A man from the volunteer fire department joined them. As they were chatting he suggested that perhaps Helene would like to join the department. Helene thought she might be interested in being an EMT (emergency medical technician), but didn't really want to fight fires. She decided to inquire.

There were no women in the fire department at the time, and the men were not too enthusiastic, to say the least, about women joining. Helene was told she couldn't be just an EMT. She would have to completely join and pass all the requirements.

"I don't know if this was true, or if they thought this would scare me away. 1 told my two friends about it, and we agreed that we would try out." Being the first woman in a man's field wasn't new to Helene. She was a beach lifeguard in college, years before women were hired.

First, Helene needed a complete physical and medical clearance. The day of her exam, her neck was bothering her from the MS. She went in to the department doctor's office wearing a neck brace.

"I told him I sprained my neck playing tennis. If he heard MS, that would have been the end of it."

They were then sent for training outside of the area. "The men there were really nice and helpful. I did have trouble with a few things like crawling through the smokehouse. When they saw my concern, two of the men offered to help me through it. One man went in front of me and another behind me. They kept me sandwiched in

Helene standing, far right, learning to use the Jaws of Life.

between them and I got through it all right."

All three women passed the physical training part. Helene went on to get her EMT certification and the advanced EMT certification.

The men in the department were not thrilled about women being there and let them know it. One night they were told that there would be important training films. It was mandatory that they be there and stay for the whole film.

"We were naive and did as we were told."

The "training films" turned out to be porno movies. The girls turned to each other as the movies started. Helene signaled for them to be quiet and to stay to the end as instructed.

"I didn't want to leave early, and give them anything to hold against us. I figured it best to follow orders and then do something about it later. Those films were disgusting, though. As I sat there waiting for them to end, I was thinking of how to get back at them."

The next day, Helene went to an adult shop and bought some magazines. With the help of the other women, she cut out pictures of male genitals.

"There was one for every man in the dept. We pasted them on the walls throughout the place, and gave each one a name of one of the firemen."

When the men saw the pictures, they immediately removed them, but never said a word. "I guess they were afraid of what we might do next. One man, who felt very strongly about not having women there, did complain to headquarters, but got nowhere. Whoever heard the complaint must have known what they had done and ignored him. If something like that happened today we could have had a big suit of sexual harassment."

The women stayed on. Helene was in the department for six years. "Once we showed the men that we were as good as they were, and that they could count on us when we were fighting fires, they treated us as equals. I guess we earned their respect. Besides that, we had the medical certification that most of them didn't have, so they really needed us."

In the beginning there were no uniforms to fit the women. They had to bring their own boots and slickers. "I had the silliest looking yellow boots that I wore. They served the purpose until our uniforms came."

Helene's first fire was some introduction to the department. She and her friends carried around pagers so they knew when they were needed. They heard there was a fire in Point Lookout and rushed to the scene. "We were the first ones there and the chief groaned 'Oh, Shit,' when he saw us and only us."

"It was a small fire in a house and we managed to put it out quickly. However, when we got clearance to leave, the fire really wasn't completely out. During the night it flared up again."

This time the fire was out of control and departments from all over were called in to help. Helene was stationed outside with the hoses to keep the fire from spreading to the neighboring homes. "I was up all night. When I finally finished, they had to chop the ice off me."

Helene knew someone was rescued from inside the house, but didn't learn until the next day, that it was a young man of 23, and he died. That really shook her up. She went to the wake along with the other firemen.

"At first it was so exciting, like a childhood fantasy riding around in the fire truck with the sirens blasting, but that first fire and the death made us all realize the seriousness of what we were doing."

For the most of her participation in the department, though, Helene did more of the medical end than fighting fires, which is what she really wanted to do. "It was a great feeling to be helping people, and in some cases knowing you saved their lives."

On one call that Helene responded to there was a young girl on the ground with a head injury and couldn't move her leg. There was intense training about staying calm and keeping parents calm and it became routine to keep your head together no matter what you saw. Except this one time. The girl was Helene's daughter and Helene became a typical hysterical mother.

"I screamed when I realized it was Jennifer and went into a panic. I couldn't treat her. Someone else had to. The others were calming me down the way I was trained to calm others."

Helene called George who met her at the hospital. Jennifer had a fractured skull. Although it wasn't properly diagnosed right away, she was O.K.

There were many funny instances also. One of the three women really was a klutz. One time while driving the ambulance she backed up into a motorcycle. Another time she slipped into the bushes where the fire was spreading and had to be rescued. Once, when Helene had spent some time calming down a heart attack patient, she loudly burst into the room with a loud "Ta Da. I'm here!" giving everyone a jolt. Eventually, she was asked to resign.

"After six years, it got to me," Helene said. "I saw too much blood and tragedy. After the last big car accident. I just felt it was time for me to leave."

# FOND MEMORIES
# AND NOT SO FOND

Each marathon that Helene ran has its own story. Most of the experiences were good ones.

Helene's favorite marathons were in Maine. "There were less runners there and the people were so nice. They really went out of their way for the Achilles runners."

It was in one of the Maine marathons that Helene took first place of all in her age group, not just first place in the disabled division. In Maine she also tied her best time of 4 hours and 15 minutes. "The course in Maine is very hilly which makes it harder, but the countryside is so beautiful."

In Maine they had medical tents set up as in the other marathons. Only here Helene noticed as she ran by that they were empty. In other marathons there is almost always someone being treated for one thing or another. "Most of the Maine runners were very experienced and didn't need any medical attention."

Later on in the race, however, she noticed that there were people being treated in the tents and they were all from the Achilles Club. "What a fine example we are setting," Helene cajoled to Dick. George was in one of the tents as well. He still continues to throw up whenever he runs a marathon.

One embarrassing incident that Helene can laugh at now occurred in the 1996 New York City Marathon. Helene was running along with her male volunteers and suddenly started bleeding from the vaginal area. Helene was so focused on the race that she didn't even realize it, although everyone else around her did. Her male volunteers were too embarrassed to say any thing to her even after some blood began to splash on to their clothes. Finally, a man ran by and in a strong English accent informed her, "you are having your period." Helene looked down at her bloody clothes and was mortified. She was also scared because it was not time for her menstrual period. "Why didn't you say something?" she yelled to the volunteers.

"We didn't want to embarrass you. We didn't know what to do."

She went to the medical tent and put on a silverfoil cape that runners are given after a race. She also had a blood blister on her foot. They wanted her to go to the hospital immediately, but of course Helene refused. They popped the blister, and she completed the race. Meanwhile, George was following his standard procedure, throwing up during this whole fiasco.

Helene questioned her son, now a gynecologist, but he was too uncomfortable to talk about this with his own mother. "Call your doctor. I don't know what it is." It turned out to be nothing serious. Her doctor cauterized it and Helene and everyone tried to forget the whole thing. "Now I look back and can laugh at it."

One of Helene's adventures that wasn't so pleasant was when she joined the World Teams Bike Tour in 1994. This is a tour that bikes around the world. Helene decided to try one leg of the trip, from Washington D.C. to Boston. After Boston, the bikers would be flown to Europe to continue. The trip was to take two weeks. Helene trained hard for it. They told her she should be able to maintain at least a 10 m.p.h. speed and be able to do this for a whole day. The trip covered about 100 miles a day. "I was able to do this, and felt prepared for the event."

When Helene arrived in Washington, there was nobody there to greet her at the airport as promised. "Here

I was all alone in a strange city and it felt weird. When I got to the hotel where I was supposed to stay in a private room, there weren't any available. I should have realized then that this wasn't going to be a good trip."

Helene was eventually given a room with two lesbians and felt very awkward. "I knew they didn't want me there. I felt like I was intruding. They knew each other from before and came on the trip together."

On the first morning, everybody started out together. "I couldn't believe how fast everyone was going. There was a man there with one leg on a regular bike and he just flew. I couldn't keep up."

One of the crew yelled to me, "Hines, muscle up!"

"I was the slowest one there on a regular bike."

The next day the bikers were put in groups with the slowest ones starting out ahead. Helene was in the slowest group. "I wasn't used to that," she admitted.

In fact she was the only regular bike in her group. The others were using wheel chairs or handcranked chairs. The people all seemed to know each other from previous events and were cliquey. The fast bikers didn't associate with the slower ones.

"I didn't know anyone and didn't find anyone to buddy up with."

The countryside was very scenic, but the weather was horrible for most of the trip so it was unpleasant. "It is hard to enjoy beautiful scenery in the pouring rain."

At the end of each day, they discarded their biking uniforms and had to dress for a formal dinner. "I would much have preferred to be eating in a casual outfit rather than dressing up each night."

There were a couple of private rooms available, but not every night. So they assigned them on a rotating basis. "The night it was my turn, I felt so relieved. Just to have a room to myself and totally relax. I couldn't wait for the

Helene with volunteer on World Teams Bike Tour. 1994

Helene, George and volunteers at New York City Marathon. 1997

trip to end."

When they did arrive in Boston, Helene's son was there to greet her. They wanted to have a special celebration for that last night, but Helene just wanted out. "I told Brian I was staying with him whether he liked it or not."

One good result of that tour was when she met Dick Hoyt. He joined the group near Boston. Hoyt runs and bikes, pulling or pushing his paralyzed son. He has done marathons and even triathalons this way. "He is quite a guy, and I am glad I got to have met him."

Another event that Helene found frustrating was the United States Games for the Disabled. Helene trained for a lot of different events that were new to her like javelin and discus and power lifting. "I'm competitive and trained hard for the event, but I really didn't have to. In trying to be fair, they had a lot of different categories. For some of the events I was the only one in my category and I got a gold medal. The power-lifting event didn't even take place. A doctor examines the competitors before the event and he told me I couldn't run more than a 5K even though I told him I had run marathons. The idea of the games is a good one, but I never went back."

On the whole though, Helene enjoyed all her adventures and triumphs. Even those races that were a terrible struggle gave her a great feeling afterwards.

# TWO STEPS BACK; ONE STEP FORWARD

Helene continued with her health relatively stable for the next few years. From 1990 to 1998 she ran 27 marathons and numerous other races. The various MS attacks would come and go and she was learning to live with them. She continued her therapy, physical workouts and part time work. In the New York City marathon of 1998 she thought she would try to beat her best time and try to break four hours.

That marathon developed into a real struggle. Looking back, Helene says, "I just should have stopped".

She and her group stuck it out and she did finish, but with a time of 4 hours and 25 minutes. During the race, Helene felt dizzy. She would stop to rest, but as soon as she ran the dizziness returned. Her volunteers held her and encouraged her. The dizzy spells led to nausea. This never happened before, and as in all the previous setbacks, she ignored the feelings as much as possible and finished the race.

She rested the next few days, waiting for the dizziness to go away. As with all the other physical ailments from her illness, Helene knew it wasn't permanent and she would wait it out. When she did feel better and began to run, the dizziness started again. After a few times she reported this to her doctor. He prescribed a new medicine to relieve it.

Helene questioned, "Am I aggravating the condition with all my running?"

The doctor told her, "No," so she decided to continue as in the past.

However, this time was different. Whenever Helene ran, she immediately became dizzy and nauseous. The last time she ran she was on the Long Beach boardwalk with George and a friend. She had allowed some time to go by for the medicine to take its effect, if it was going to help, and went out for one more try. After a short distance, she stopped. "I can't do this," she was forced to admit to herself with despair.

George, in his encouraging way, told her to take it slow. "Let's try just one more block at an easy pace."

"No, George. I just can't do it."

She was so emphatic about the way she said it and there were tears in her eyes. George stopped frozen. He didn't know what to say. Helene never said "can't." In fact there was no such word as "can't." Numerous articles were already written about this amazing woman and how she was conquering MS. This was scary to him and devastating to Helene. She had triumphed over unbelievable odds, but now had to admit defeat.

They were quiet on the way home. George wanted to console her, but didn't know what to say. Helene went home and cried and fell into a depression. She had fought with all her might to walk and then run. Now she couldn't run anymore, even short distances, let alone a marathon., and the fear of the future was looming heavy on her.

One day, while she was going through this, Dick called. "I have something you might be interested in," he said with enthusiasm in his voice. "It is a hand cranked chair, somewhat of a cross between a wheel chair and a bike. I know you will like it."

She called Bob Hall in Boston who made these devices. After some discussion, Helene decided to order one. George had a convention in Rhode Island where Bob had a distributor, so Helene went with him to get the chair. The representative showed Helene how to use it.

"It took a while to get used to it, but I knew this was for me."

She took the chair home with her, and started riding the boardwalk in Long Beach. "It felt so good to be mobile again. I could go fast without getting dizzy and it was a good workout for my upper body."

The hand-cranker looks like a wheel chair from the back, but the seat is very low to the ground. There is another wheel in front. Sometimes this wheel is smaller than the others. Extending off the sides of the front wheel are bars to rest the feet. To operate it, one sits with legs straight out in front, feet resting in the bars while the hands are holding the "pedals." The "pedals" are really small handles. They are connected to a gear wheel which is attached by bars to the front wheel. The gear wheel has a chain that connects it to the rear gear wheel just as in a bicycle. There are also hand brakes and shift levers or buttons that operate the way a bicycle does. The chair is propelled by pushing and pulling on the pedal handles with the hands and arms. This part is different from a bike, because both handles work together, not one up and one down as in a bike. Both hands push forward, and then pull back.

With practice, Helene soon mastered the chair. Her spirits went up. She started different workouts to increase her arm strength to get better speed and to increase her stamina. Dick suggested that she enter the next marathon with it. Helene said, "Why not?"

The next New York City marathon was coming up in a few months and Helene trained hard for it as usual. Once again, she had goals to make her workouts more meaningful and was able to exercise again. Helene finished first place in the women's wheel chair division of the 1999 marathon and felt great. In subsequent marathons Helene beat the men as well as the women.

# The Hand-Crank Racer: Built for Speed and Comfort

A hand-crank or hand-cycle wheelchair is typically made of chrome-moly steel or aluminum, weighs about 28 pounds and costs $2,900 to $5,000. It can travel up to 25 miles an hour. A hand-crank allows for a more comfortable seating position than that of a push-rim wheelchair. The rider remains erect and pedals with a smooth arm motion. This is easier on the shoulders than leaning forward and using the hands to rotate the wheels of a push-rim.

**THE RIDE**
Riders choose gears depending on their strength and mobility. They use their biceps, triceps and laterals to create a push-pull motion on the hand crank that powers the wheelchair. Either the hands or legs may be used to steer. Squeezing the brake lever stops the wheelchair.

**WHEELS**
Skinny tubular wheels made of carbon fiber are the wheels of choice for racing. Rear wheels are tilted inward to increase speed.

**GEARS**
21 gears.

**BRAKE/ SHIFTER COMBO**

**HAND CRANKS**
Some are molded to allow the fingers to fit into them. Wrists can also be tied to them if there is a problem with the hands.

**BRAKES**
Center-pull, placed on the front wheel because most of the rider's weight is carried over the front wheel.

**WATER BOTTLE**

**SEAT**

**DERAILLEUR**

**FOOTREST**

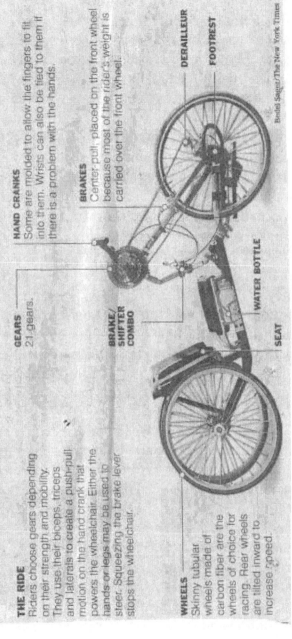

Bedel Saget/The New York Times

64

Helene receives the Key to the City. 2003.

Her win stirred up some controversy because of the hand-cranked wheelchair. Some said that it is not a wheel chair, and should not be allowed in the wheel chair division, but should have its own separate division. This controversy is still going on. In some races there are separate categories for wheelchair and hand-cranked wheelchairs. In others, the hand-cranks are allowed to participate, but only as an exhibition event, and get no recognition at all. Helene is trying to change this. "I would like to see the hand-cranked wheelchairs get the recognition they need. They are less taxing on the body than racing in wheelchairs that can cause carpal tunnel and other problems, but physically still very demanding. In the future, if they get the recognition, I can see more and more people using them. They are fun for recreational use, too."

Thrilled with her victory, Helene entered upcoming marathons just like before, She is still doing so today, and has come in first in every one of them.

There are times though when it is hard, One day her son, Brian, was with her in a park. To look at Helene, one would never know the daily battle she is up against. "People without MS have no idea what you are going through."

Seeing her doing so well Brian offered to run with her a short distance if she wanted to try. Helene's heart sank. "I wish I could, but you don't understand, Brian, I just can't. Please don't ask me anymore. It hurts." He never asked her again.

Helene now rides the hand-cranked chair every chance she gets. She also continues to kayak which is fun and a good cross training for her arms.

# ANALOGY OF MS

One cold winter day while we were biking on the boardwalk and looking at the ocean, we spotted a few surfers. Helene knew that I sometimes surf in the winter, and she asked me about how the suit can possibly keep me warm.

I explained to her that you don't feel the cold like you do when you're outdoors without a coat. You don't sit there shivering, but eventually you do get cold. It is gradual. The first time I was out in winter with a friend who got me started on winter surfing, we talked as he gave me pointers. After a while, our lips and cheeks got numb and we began slurring our words like a drunk and had to stop talking. Later, I would find myself slowing down, although I did not realize it. I would be paddling in slow motion though it felt normal and I would miss a wave. Then when I did catch a wave, I would fall right off the board because my feet were becoming numb and I could not balance on the board.

Helene turned to me and profoundly said, "Now you know what it feels like to have MS."

"That's awful," I replied, but continued to think of those words for a long time. That she feels everyday what I feel when I get cold in the ocean. It is hard to put yourself in someone else's shoes, or experience exactly what they are feeling, but I think that simple analogy did it for me.

One of the most difficult things with MS is that it is so unpredictable. People living with the illness never know what to expect. It can affect almost any part of the body. When a person without it wakes up to a stiff neck they attribute it to the way they slept and think nothing of it.

A person with MS wakes up to a stiff neck, and fears that this is the beginning of another attack. A prime example of this was Helene's reaction to when the lights when out.

She was teaching a large class in the high school pool for adult education one Halloween night. Suddenly, as a result of a local blackout, everything went completely dark. Due to the location of the pool, it was like being in a forest and not being able to see your hand in front of your face. Everyone realized the lights went out and got nervous because of it.

Helene, instead, screamed to her friend, "Oh, my God. I've gone blind. I can't see anything." Panic filled her voice. When she realized it wasn't the MS causing her to lose her vision, she felt so relieved and took control of the situation to calm everybody down. "Everyone was frightened, but as long as I knew it wasn't my eyes, I felt there was nothing to be upset about. I remained calm and in turn that kept everyone else calm."

"I was in the shallow water, and called out for everyone to softly call to each other and reach for someone's hand. If they were deep they could follow the sound of my voice to the shallow end and all should keep going hand in hand until they reached a wall of the pool. Then they could help each other out or just hang on to the edge. I knew they couldn't be too far from one of the walls of the pool."

When Helene felt that everybody was safe (there were close to 60 people in the class), she and the other instructor who knew the area well, felt their way to the nearest phone. They called 911 and returned to the pool to tell people that help was on the way. However, as time went on, the people began to get restless and nervous. Finally, a young man in the building heard the commotion and came to the pool. He was using only matches to light the way. He stayed until everybody was safely out of the pool area and recovered their belongings and coats. They then made a human chain and left the building. The police never came.

When Helene called the police to find out why they hadn't come, they told her that because it was Halloween, they thought it was just another prank call.

"I was furious. How could they not even check out a call like that from an adult? Even if they called the school, they would have been told there was a local blackout. Fortunately, no one was hurt."

Helene did make a lot of other calls. She was told that auxiliary emergency lights were not mandatory although that made no sense to her.

"There was no reason to sue, as we were all O.K. I just didn't want anything like that to happen again."

I am sure that by the time Helene finished the conversation, the police would never again ignore another call.

# AT LAST, AN MS CLASS

Helene kept up with her exercise program on land and especially in the water. She knew how much it was helping her and wanted to continue the water exercise classes for people with MS that she had originally started. She was constantly looking to pick up where she left off. It always bothered her, after having started the class, having seen results and then having to end it.

One day, Larry Elovich, a prominent lawyer in Long Beach, told her of a new place that was going to open up in the city. It was to be a state of the art gym and rehab center with pools. Helene found the new owner who was currently working at a rehab across the street. Doctors offices would be on the third floor, a regular gym on the second floor, and pools on the ground floor. The place would be run as a regular gym open to members, as well as a place where doctors could prescribe therapy for their patients. There would be several pools. One would be a 75-foot lap pool for laps and exercise classes. Next to that would be a smaller therapy pool with treadmills, stationery bicycles and other equipment in the water. This pool would be a warmer temperature and be open to members and be used for patients prescribed for water therapy. There would also be a hot tub and three current pools of different depths. The current could be adjusted manually to provide resistance. Helene was very excited about this new place and spoke to him of her plans.

She explained what she wanted to do with the MS classes. She offered to teach other classes at the center if he would allow the MS classes to be held there. Expenses would be paid by the MS society for the use of the place.

One of the first classes at the Sunrise Center.

MS water class, with volunteers, taking a break.

Eventually, he agreed. She took him to another therapy center in the area that she was affiliated with so she could show him what she needed. The people there angrily accused her of bringing in a spy to the place, as if she was trying to do them one better and take their clients away.

"That was ridiculous. He could have gone there on his own without me. They didn't have anywhere near the same kind of setup that he was planning. I just wanted to give him an idea of what I intended to do."

The center was due to open in several months. Months went by, but nothing. There were all kind of problems holding it up. Each time Helene asked, "When?" he would answer, "Soon."

A year and half later the Sunrise Center in Long Beach, (now Park Avenue Fitness) was open. Before the MS class was scheduled, Helene started teaching water aerobics classes there to familiarize herself with the facility.

Meanwhile, Helene was getting opposition from the head of the MS society. He said there were already a few pools in the area open to people with MS. Helene was exasperated. "Those pools don't offer what I am going to offer. They just allow people to go in the pools on their own, and walk around in the water. I am going to give them a complete body workout that is better than therapy. These people desperately need this."

There was a lot of haggling back and forth.

"Perhaps we'll try a pilot program," it was suggested.

"No, we are doing this," Helene insisted.

Finally, it was announced in the MS newsletter that on July 4th, 1999, Helene would hold her first MS class at the center. They were scheduled for Monday nights and Thursday mornings. The classes were immediately successful, and friends began to tell friends. The pool was accessible with walkers, and there was a chair lift for those in wheel chairs. Some people first came to observe, a little unsure of the class, and then once they saw what it was like, quickly joined.

One woman had heard about Helene and the classes and came to check it out. She saw "this lady built like a brick shit house." (Others, including George, have described Helene this way). After the initial intimidation though, the visitor became a regular at the class. She started out for only twenty minutes and then was so tired she used the chair lift to leave the pool. Now she stays the whole hour, only uses the stairs, and went from fear of the deep water to ending the class doing laps.

The owner did send down a personal trainer and a massage therapist when they were free to help out. However, the classes were getting larger, and Helene knew she needed more help to properly and safely run them. It also really bothered her to have to cancel a class when she was away, and she often left the area to do her marathons and other races. That is where I came in to the picture.

Helene was practicing with her hand-cranked chair on the boardwalk. She stopped to talk to many people who questioned her about the type of "bike" she was using, or once they knew her to congratulate her on her recent accomplishments.

One day, she happened to talk to a friend of mine. "She was so nice," my friend recalled. "When she realized I was alone for the Jewish holidays, she invited me to go to temple with her and George." During the course of the conversation my name came up as someone who might be able to help her. I had just retired from teaching physical education. School had reopened and I felt a little lost. The novelty of being free had worn off, and I needed something to do. This wasn't exactly what I originally had in mind for volunteer work, but it was local, and in my field, so I decided to give it a try.

The first time I visited the Center was on a Thursday

morning. There were about 10 people in the class. Helene beckoned me to "come play with us," and I jumped in. Although physical education was my background, I was unfamiliar with water therapy, but I could tell that Helene was trying to get these people to use and develop all their muscles, and to put their joints through the full range of movement as with land workouts. I was impressed with the workout she was giving them. I watched and learned as I participated.

I didn't know much about MS at the time, and the people in the class all seemed O.K. in the water. They moved about quite freely. It wasn't until after class was over, when I saw them leave the pool, did I realize their condition. As they climbed the steps to get out of the pool, they would stiffen as soon as their body began to leave the water.. Some dragged a foot, others reached for their walkers or canes. It was amazing how much they could do in the water in spite of the difficulty they had trying to walk and balance on land.

Helene did a lot of work for balance and proper walking. Many of them drag one foot on land, but in the water they could do a natural walk with each foot, weight shifting from heel to toe. After that, there were foam dumbbells that provide a lot of resistance in the water. They are used for strength training, much like weights on land. Helene tried to vary the activities from class to class to make it more interesting and fun, but part of each class was spent with safety belts in the deep water. With the body completely suspended in the deep water, many movements could be accomplished that could not be done anywhere else.

The pool also had apparatus called aquatrends that were connected to the side of the pool. These had high handles for uses with the hands over head as in pull-ups, and low handles for work with arms low such as pike leg lifts. There are so many exercises that can be done on these that would be extremely difficult if not impossible out of the water.

The class was supposed to be held in the main lap pool, but there were times when the class was small and the therapy pool was empty and Helene moved the class into the therapy pool for the last twenty minutes or so. There they could use exercise bikes and treadmills that were under water. Sometimes, they could also use the current pools where the force of the current could be controlled. Helene and I would divide the class up to give more individual attention to each person. Half might go deep with me for one type of workout, and then we would switch. My half of the class would go to Helene, and her group would come deep with me. At the end, we all performed an activity together and stretched together as a class.

Helene convinced me to join her on Monday nights as well. Most of the participants in the evening came to the class after work and were a little punchy by a day at the office. After class, most of them would go out to dinner and over a period of time became a close knit group of friends. I came regularly on Thursdays and Mondays, and covered the classes for her when she was away. She also recruited volunteers whenever she could.

One day, Alan, semi-retired from the computer business met Helene in the local bagel shop. He offered to help, and became a Monday night regular.

The Monday night dinners became a big attraction to the class. Some people joined us at the restaurant when for one reason or another they couldn't exercise with the group, just to meet their friends for dinner. Linda, the dinner organizer, became extremely efficient. Most restaurants couldn't accommodate a large group quickly on Mondays and no one wanted to stay too late on a work night. It was usually a slow night when restaurants had less help. Linda would arrive in class with menus, have everybody make a choice and phone in the orders. Then with the help of Alan, and her pretty colored calculator, would individualize the bill for each person. Sometimes she would get specials from the restaurants for our business. They might provide free salads or desserts or beverages.

The atmosphere Helene created in the classes was extremely upbeat. In the water the people laughed and socialized, acted silly at times, but came away with a great workout. I admired how well they had adjusted to this debilitating illness that had changed their lives. When the classes were small, Helene and I would "gang up" on someone, giving him or her complete attention. It was in this way that we got one of the women in the deep end. She was a little unsure of herself, because, although a good swimmer at one time, she couldn't keep her body under control. Helene got behind her and said, "Do you want to go all the way to the far wall at the 7 foot end?"

She shook her head, but I came in front and grabbed her hand and told her, "You don't have a choice," while Helene held her waist. Helene gently encouraged her and assured her that we both had her as we slowly moved towards the wall. Had she begun to panic or gotten upset, Helene would not have continued, but because of the way Helene handled it, she began to laugh. When she reached the wall she smiled, looked at the two of us and said in her cute way, a line she often used, "Another fine mess you got me into."

Within a few weeks Helene had everybody at the far end and I brought my camera to take a picture as proof. One woman remarked, "My husband will never believe this." After additional time, even those who were initially afraid managed to go deep on their own with the use of a safety belt; others began to swim laps without the use of a belt.

Next, Helene decided everyone should learn how to swim, so each class ended with swimming practice. Helene would not take no for an answer, and soon those who were reluctant to get their hair wet were swimming laps. It was great the way Helene could relate to them. When she told them to try something, and they would respond, ". . .but you don't understand," and go on about their pain or lack of use of an arm or a leg, Helene could remind them that she had MS herself, and yes she certainly did understand.

Then they might comment, "But you are a super athlete. You ran marathons." When they heard she had started the marathons after she was diagnosed with MS, and that there was a time when she couldn't walk, they would just stare at this woman, dumbfounded.

Helene has become such an inspiration to everyone with or without MS.

# REACHING OUT TO OTHERS

Helene was asked to speak at an MS support group and asked me to join her. She insisted that the main reason for my going was to give a different perspective on how the water therapy was helping. She also asked that I run the VCR when she was showing different videos. Later I teased her that running the VCR was my main reason for being invited. Helene is quite mechanically disabled. She touches something and it "breaks." She thinks I'm so great because I can fix it, but the truth is, it was never really broken in the first place. She just didn't know how to operate it.

Once she asked me to figure out why her back seat wouldn't go all the way down. "If you can get it to go down, my chair will fit in." I "fixed" it by moving the object out of the way that was blocking it. She just smiled and laughed at herself.

However, it was at that support group meeting that I began to learn Helene's story. She showed slides and videos of people with severe handicaps who still managed to participate in athletic events. She explained how she was paralyzed and then learned to walk and run. It was so inspiring to listen to her. Although what she spoke about was sad, it was inspiring, not depressing to listen to. She encouraged her audience to join our water classes and had me speak of the improvement I had seen. Several new people from that group did come to the classes after the meeting.

When I heard Helene was to be honored at the local Chamber of Commerce meeting one night, I, of course, attended. Several people from the class were also present.

It was there that I began to realize even more what an amazing woman Helene is, and I was flattered by her interest and respect for me. The man presenting the award, Larry Elovich, spoke about Helene's accomplishments. He referred to her as a world class athlete who competed in 27 marathons as well as numerous other races while fighting MS. All the money she obtained from winning any event was always donated to a charity, the Achilles club or to obtain a wheelchair for someone that couldn't afford one. She never kept any of it.

Elovich mentioned how he foolishly accepted a challenge from Helene to have a push-up contest. "The idea that a woman could beat me in push-ups was ridiculous, but I stopped at 65 while Helene stopped at 75."

I wish I had heard this before I said I would go biking with her. I would have known what to expect.

Helene was racing very often and practiced almost everyday on the boardwalk. She liked to have company, so I said I would go when she asked me. I really didn't want to. Silly me, I thought I was doing her a favor. She was doing so much for others, I didn't want to say no. I consider myself a fairly good biker, and I felt it would be boring to keep at her pace, which probably would be between 8-10 miles per hour at most. Was I in for a surprise! Helene likes to average 13 miles per hour in her races, which takes in going down to about 4 on some hills. So to maintain that average overall speed, it meant that most of her straight-a-way speed was much faster than 13.

The boardwalk is flat and Helene would go about 12 miles per hour into the wind, and about 15 or more with the wind. I had trouble keeping up. My legs were burning, but I didn't want to admit it. After all, my legs were competing against her arms.

While going with the wind, I had an advantage because I could take a few hard pedals, and then "coast" which she was unable to do on the hand-crank. This gave me a little respite. Going into the wind was another story. She would get ahead of me, and yell back, "get up here," and I would push hard to keep up. Every now and then she would stop to talk to someone, or take a drink of water and I would sigh with relief.

Eventually, on future rides, 1 just gave up. I had to admit that her arms were stronger pedaling than my legs. I would let her peel out at 17 miles per hour and I would stay back and enjoy the scenery. There were times, embarrassing as it was, that I would "draft" off her during a strong head wind. (That is a term used when one biker stays close on the tail of another. The first biker blocks the wind a bit and makes it easier. Sometimes in a race, two bikers will take turns drafting off of each other). I always was ready to stop when she was, and usually before. It was only when her shoulder bothered her, that I found the ride easy. One time I was really worried because she had a bad cold and was ready to stop before I was, after only two laps. This never happened before, and it scared me, especially when she said her chest hurt. No pain ever seemed to slow her down before. I was afraid she might have pneumonia. Fortunately, she didn't, and was alright in a couple of days.

Biking wasn't something I usually did in the winter either. So between the workouts at the pool and the biking in between, I really toned up. I thought I was in good shape before, but after a few months with the maniac, as I now referred to her, without losing weight, I dropped a size in my jeans.

It was during these bike rides that this book was written. I would question Helene, she would answer and I would record it by immediately writing it down when I returned home. Bit by bit, chapter by chapter, Helene biked and told me her story. (She had the breath to speak while biking. I didn't. I just had to listen).

Helene was also teaching other classes at the pool besides going for her own therapy and workouts. A typical day for her might be teaching an hour class in the morning of water exercises, followed by the MS water class. Then she would call me to go biking, go back to the gym to teach an exercise class on land, and then another water aerobics class. When I covered her classes for her, I was wiped out. I also didn't bike in between. I slept to have energy for the evening classes.

As if all this wasn't enough, Helene decided to take boxing lessons. She wanted to improve her arm endurance and strength for the races and thought boxing would help her. She found the boxing did much, much more than that however. Her arms and abdominals did improve, but also, so did her balance and coordination. For the first time in years, she found she could jump rope. Not only that, her memory improved. Doing various sequences where she had to concentrate really helped. "I could never remember a whole bunch of things at once. This was great."

So Helene continued her boxing lessons as part of her regular routine. This was about the only thing I managed to successfully avoid. She urged me to try it, but it just did not interest me at all. Then she added some of the punches into the water classes. After that, she got the brilliant idea to start an MS boxing class.

"I figured if it is good for me, it should be good for others, so I wanted to give it a shot." With all her personal problems, she is always looking to help others.

She convinced a few of her students to include boxing in their activities and the results were amazing. Two women who used walkers were so focused on the punches they began, without realizing it, to step forward towards the targets Helene was holding as she moved backwards.

Cannon, L.I. Marathon finish line. 2002.

She used spotters in case they did lose their balance. When these two women saw how far they had moved, they were shocked and thrilled.

To get more people with MS or any disability interested in boxing, she received permission to give a presentation at one of the local outdoor concerts at the beach. I was dragged along to provide the sound effects. With a boom box playing "Rocky" and other boxing music, I was backstage turning the music on and off as necessary.

Helene demonstrated how a hula hoop could be put on the ground. This gave the person a focal point within a set area. A spotter would be behind them with a hand on their back for support and to grab them should they lose their balance. People with poor balance could still reap the benefits. Even from a wheel chair, one could practice the punches. She did a great presentation, which was very difficult because she was demonstrating in the sand, which made balancing harder.

"At one point I almost fell, but somehow I managed to do it."

After the presentation, we enjoyed the rest of the concert.

# DO OR DIE

Helene started out the South Shore Jersey Marathon as she did all her other races. She was well prepared, confident, but not cocky. We had been biking a lot in the previous weeks to train for this event.

During the race, she teamed up with another man and they took turns drafting off of each other. However, after a while, Helene told him, the pace was too slow and she was going to take off on her own. She looked at the time and immediately realized she had to go faster at that point if she wanted to win. At speeds of around 20 m.p.h. she gave it her all.

Suddenly without warning, Helene was over on her side, face smashed into the road, where the helmet didn't protect her. The man behind her caught up to her, and left when he knew help was on the way. Helene waited for the ambulance, which was "soooo slow" or at least seemed that way. Helene wanted to get back on the chair and finish the race. When the ambulance did arrive, the EMC insisted she be brought to the hospital.

"Just patch me up, and get me on my chair. I've got to finish this race." Helene not only wanted to finish, but win, and time was running out.

Finally, they acquiesced, and Helene was back on the road, in her handcrank, with an escort. She told them the route, and she followed, periodically shouting to them where to turn. Blood was still coming out of her eye, skin from her cheek was hanging down, and she could hardly see. The race, when in it, is everything and Helene threw caution to the wind. She didn't come in first overall of the men and women, but she still came in first for women.

George was at the finish line and couldn't believe what

he saw. She was covered with blood, her face swollen, and although he, as a surgeon was used to seeing blood, was still taken aback.

The officials took one look at her and said, "You don't want to wait around for your award. Here, take it now and get to a doctor."

They recommended she not go to the local hospital, but to her own plastic surgeon. George drove her to a doctor, where she was stitched in two places around the eye. Fortunately, there was no serious damage to the eye, though the doctor said there could possibly be a fracture farther back.

After it was all over, it was George who felt sick and faint and had to sit with his feet up to keep from passing out. Later than night, when he did recover, he wanted to go out to eat. Helene was so embarrassed to be seen, she covered her head with a big cap with a long bill, wore large sun glasses, long sleeves, and refused to look up when a friend of George came to the table to say hello.

I went over to see her that night. The only way to describe her was the scene from Rocky after his first fight. Her eye was half shut, swollen and purple, her cheeks and lips were red with oozing blood and swollen as well. The sunglasses did hide a lot though. I told her she could still teach her classes from the poolside, (she wasn't allowed in the water until the stitches were out). As long as she wore sunglasses, it didn't look as horrible as she thought it did. But she did buy a bigger pair of wrap around glasses.

The worst part, she admitted, was that "I don't know what happened. I don't know if I hit something, or the bike behind me touched me, or what."

When you know why an accident occurred, you can then do something to prevent it in the future. I suggested she try to contact someone who was behind her who might be able to give her some clue as to what happened. One

Helene and Kyler at the finish line of the New York Marathon. 2003.

thing kept nagging at her. Just before the accident happened, "I remember saying to myself, where is the brake? Why would I say that?"

Trying to get to the bottom of what happened, Helene recalled having gotten a new medicine a few days before to help calm her hands. "It really did help me, but when we researched the drug, one of the side effects is possible disorientation. Maybe that is why I lost it for a second and couldn't find the brake."

Whatever it was, George did not want her to race again without some kind of face mask. I joked about a roll bar for the bike, a hockey or umpire mask or even a catcher's mask. Helene did not appreciate my suggestions.

That night after the Monday class when we went out to dinner, Helene had her sunglasses, big purple cap, and purple jacket. I said she looked like *Tickle Me Elmo* or *Barney.* She took the teasing in stride, and we were all glad that nothing more serious had happened. The people in the class were very upset. They felt that this time, Helene had pushed herself too far. The consensus was, "she should have left the race and gone in the ambulance. Winning isn't that important."

The trophy she received was really beautiful. Mounted on three tiers of wood was a lighthouse with a gold plaque announcing her first place.

Helene was not going to stay off her chair. A few days later she had a new helmet purchased from a local bike shop. It had a shield that came down over her face, and attached to the bottom was a piece that protruded like a jawbone, giving her face complete protection. Thursday, after the MS class, she put on her new helmet and took a young man out to the boardwalk to teach him how do to the handcrank. And that Sunday, she did the Long Island Marathon along with a few of the people in the MS class whom she introduced to the handcranks.

Helene continued to teach the classes that week from a chair by the pool. We split up the class by ability. She took the more able bodied people who could follow her instructions from the chair. I was in the water with the others where I could assist them if needed. Nobody could believe what she looked like, and that she could still come out to do the classes.

In spite of all this, she nevertheless remembered my birthday. She got a cake for the Monday night dinner after class and another one for the Thursday class. She left the pool for a few seconds to light the cake. One of the people in the class said something was burning. The smell was getting stronger and we were nervous. I called to Helene who was in the office. She didn't answer. I shouted her name louder, really getting scared now. In case there was a fire, it would be a difficult job to get everybody out quickly. The next scream probably showed panic in my voice. I was afraid to leave the pool with the MS people in it and I couldn't get her attention.

Because of the lack of control in her hands, Helene was having trouble lighting the cake, which is what caused the burning smell. She heard me calling and tried to light the cake even faster, which caused more problems. She said to herself, "Shut up, Barb." When she did appear with the cake, everybody laughed.

After that, I did what can only be compared to a declaration of war. In a weak moment I satisfied a childhood fantasy. As I gave her a hug to thank her, I smushed a flower in the icing all over her cheek.

This had actually started a few months before when Helene bought a cake for dinner to celebrate her own birthday. I told her that I was planning on bringing a cake. I said, "You shouldn't buy your own birthday cake"

Helene felt she wanted to do it. I suggested she pick out what she wanted, but I would pay for it. A few hours later, I got an S.O.S. from her. In the process of putting the cake in the car and taking things out, she lost her balance and fell forward. She was fine, but there was a huge dent in the cake box, which in turn left a huge dent in the cake. She was too busy to get another one, so as I had originally planned, I bought a cake.

At the dinner we brought both cakes. Once again, laughing at herself, Helene felt the messed up cake was perfect for dinner with a group of people with MS. Balance was one of their biggest problems – they could all relate to the cake story. Everyone smiled and got a nice firm slice of the intact cake, and a flower or whatever they chose from the smushed cake.

However, looking at the messed up cake, Helene and I got the same idea to relive the old slapstick humor days and have a cake fight. We each grabbed a piece, challenged the other to throw first, and then behaving as two mature adults in a nice restaurant, we did put the pieces back on the table. However, the idea was still in our minds, and seeing the cake there at the pool I lost control.

Too weak to fight back at the time, she vowed to retaliate. Knowing she would not take this lying down, I began to watch my back at every turn. Now and then she would remind me that she hadn't forgotten. Antagonizing the "maniac" was not one of the smartest things I ever did.

# ANOTHER TWO STEPS BACK, ONE STEP FORWARD

It was recommended that Helene go for an MRI to check her liver because of the medication she was on. The new doctor she was seeing told her that some research showed that this should be standard procedure. Helene went for the MRI without giving it much thought.

Thursday night she and George went out to dinner. "He was acting very strange that night," is the way Helene described the evening. "I couldn't put my finger on it. I figured he just had some work problems that he didn't want to talk about."

The next morning he called her to come into the hospital for a CAT scan. "What do I need a CAT scan for?" she asked.

George said something wasn't right and insisted she come in for the scan. When she arrived, George greeted her with tears in his eyes. He didn't want to ruin the dinner the night before and managed to contain his tears then, but now they flowed. While checking the liver, a suspicious growth appeared on one of her kidneys. The CAT scan confirmed a cancerous tumor, although Helene had no symptoms at all. The kidney was scheduled to be removed the following Thursday.

I was waiting for Helene to call me that afternoon to go riding. When she did call and told me the news, I thought I misunderstood. When she made it clear, I was shocked and speechless for a moment. Then I tried to console her with things like "maybe it is nothing." Or other inane remarks to comfort her like "well just because there is something there doesn't mean it is cancer. Maybe it won't require surgery, etc." Of course these words were useless. Her husband was a surgeon.

She told me, "They know for sure. George was there. He saw the results. I'm going to have my kidney removed next week."

I was at a loss for words at that point. She told me there were some other tests to be done. She had to tell her children and get things in order. She really didn't want to deal with people now and asked me to cover her classes for her. I told her to call me if there was anything I could do.

The hardest thing was telling the people in the classes. "Where is Helene? Is she all right?"

I responded "No" and my tears flowed. Usually when Helene was not at a class, she was competing in some marathon or other race. Those who took the news the hardest, of course, were those in the MS class. They sat there frozen or cried. There was no easy way to break that kind of news. Helene is a role model to all, but especially to them. If she can do it, then maybe I can to, is the feeling she gives to them. If she is going down, then everyone was vulnerable. I believe they felt terrible for her to be going through this, but that it personally scared them, too. I told them she didn't want calls, but that I would inform them of her progress after the operation.

That Monday night the class still went out for dinner, but the mood was somber. It was agreed by all that classes would continue and I would be a temporary sit-in for Helene.

"The last thing Helene would want would be for us to stop working out," one of them said and they all agreed.

I had a sports catalog that one of the men wanted to look at. As he thumbed through it he came across a page of cute rubber duckies. We kidded about having them at the pool; I said I would order them. When Helene came back for her first class, we would turn them loose in the pool. After a while the mood changed a bit. We said nothing could get Helene down. She would probably be back teaching next week. It was a way to cheer each other.

The worst day for Helene after being informed of the kidney cancer was when she had the bone scan. All tests were coming back negative, which meant the cancer had not spread. When she got the bone scan, she was asked if she ever bad any broken bones. Broken bones can cause marks on the bone scan like a spreading cancer. Helene responded "No." The bone scan did reveal some marks.

Then Helene lost it. "I don't want the surgery. If it has spread just let me die now!" she cried out. "Where is George? Get him here!"

George came in and the radiologist was called. A chest x-ray was taken and it seems that Helene definitely did have some broken ribs at one time, although she didn't remember it. Fortunately, they had caused the marks on the scan. Another mark on her shoulder, George confirmed was from another injury.

When she returned home, she called me, "I just had the worst morning of my life," and described the events at the scanning. Helene was still worried that George, who kept it from her that night at dinner, might not be telling her the whole truth that everything was negative. She was still concerned.

I couldn't do much at this time but be there to listen and send her cheerful notes or e-mails. The day before the surgery she felt she wanted and needed to ride. I went with her. Doctors wanted her to rest, but mentally she had to get out. The biggest problem with the surgery was her fluctuating blood pressure, which had to be stabilized for the operation. Except for saying that I was with her for her last ride before the surgery and that she wanted me to be there for the first ride after the surgery, we spoke of everything else but the operation. Anything to keep her mind off it. Those few days seemed like an eternity, of waiting and worrying.

I called again later that night, but she was asleep, and told George to just tell her that "I am looking forward to our next bike ride."

The surgery was scheduled for ten o'clock the next morning, the time of the MS class. Some of the people there, who had not attended the Monday class, still did not know of the crisis in Helene's life. Once again, I explained what was happening. I told them she was due to be operated at that very moment, and suggested a moment of silent prayer at the poolside.

That night I waited anxiously for a call. I didn't want to bother George who had my name on a must call list, but by nine that evening I couldn't stand it. I called and heard the most wonderful news that all went well. George said he had called me and got a machine, but it wasn't mine. She was in recovery and doing fine.

I called the MS phone chain to spread the news and then waited until Saturday to call and see if she was up for phone calls or visits yet.

George said. "She may be home tomorrow." I was delighted by this good news.

Helene did indeed make an amazing recovery, typical of what the maniac would do. The hardest day was right after the surgery when she felt completely miserable. "My family was there trying to help me sit up and move, but I didn't want to do anything. I yelled at them to just leave me alone. I wasn't at all cooperative."

Jack, one of the men in the MS class who was a volunteer at that hospital, came by often. "He was so nice. When I was in my really bitchy mood, he just sat there and held my hand without saying a word."

Helene's surgery was in a teaching hospital and young residents were there to watch and learn. The surgeon told her later that when he opened her up, she was like a picture from an anatomy text. Usually there is some yellow fat over the kidneys and this is what surgeons use as a "landmark" to locate them. While the surgeon was telling this to the residents, there was no yellow fat to be found. The organs were completely visible, just like in a textbook.

At home, she was naturally weak and sore. Anxious to get back in shape again, she did everything the doctor allowed, and probably then some. We went for short walks at first, and then longer ones. She would call me up and say, "Come walk your dog."

After a week of this, she made a surprise visit to the Monday class and treated everyone to pizzas there, instead of going out to a restaurant for dinner.

When the doctor said she could exercise as long as she didn't use her abdominal muscles, Helene began to work out at the gym. She especially wanted to build up her arms for the handcrank again. Then she resumed leading her classes from the poolside. As planned 12 rubber duckies were turned loose in the pool. Each one was a different character, such as cowboy, scuba diver, etc. Helene cracked up and the class was totally disrupted. Everyone was more interested in the ducks. There were duck races and other silly games as if the class was full of children instead of adults. Everyone was just so happy to have Helene back.

Shortly after that she got the thumbs-up sign from the doctor for that promised first ride on the boardwalk. We talked about how glad we were that the surgery was behind her and about how we had felt during that last ride before the operation. A month had now passed since then.

She received a letter from the New York City Marathon from Bob Laufer, saying that she was given first seating in the New York Marathon coming up.

"What a time to get this. I always wanted it, but now I can't enter it," she said.

She kept bringing this up, and then one day she said, "Maybe I can enter it. There is still several weeks to go before the race. Maybe I can."

I told her she was ridiculous for even considering it. "You made an excellent recovery from a serious operation. There will be many other races to enter. Don't push yourself now. You just had a very serious operation. Your body is still in shock. Give yourself time so you don't do any further damage, etc. etc."

My words fell on deaf ears. She agreed not to push herself. She would start to bike as soon as the doctor told her, and take it from there.

I spoke to George. "Should she be doing this"? I asked him with worry in my voice.

"No, she shouldn't, but I can't stop her," was his answer.

I could only remind her that when she gets in a race she gets so competitive and would push herself too hard to win even without even realizing it.

The race was a week and a half away. Helene had been good about doing what the doctor had permitted. Now that she could do everything, she figured she could build up to the 26 miles in the handcrank. So the bike rides on the boardwalk became workouts again. Helene who was in such terrific shape before the operation, very quickly got back into it again. She entered the marathon and finished first in the woman's division. Usually she finishes first overall beating out the men, but not being completely in her prime, one man did beat her.

The local news did a before-and-after the race interview with her. Major TV news stations called her. The mayor invited her to get the key to the city. The Achilles Club honored her at their dinner.

"Wow", I exclaimed as one honor after the other kept coming in. "Next step is Hollywood. They will make a movie about you, and a book. Don't forget your old friends."

A little later I thought about it. "You know, I like to write. I could write your story." And so bit by bit I interviewed her as we road the boardwalk. Every one in the class was excited about the book. As I learned more about Helene, I would share it with some of the people in the class.

At first I would type it on the computer and print it out. Later, I e-mailed it to her, and printed it out after all the corrections were made for that chapter. This was a lot more difficult than it sounds.

Helene had a lap top computer without a regular mouse. It was very difficult for her to operate it with the problems MS was causing in her fingers. Here again, I realized what a big handicap she was living with. I tried to teach her and it was frustrating for her, but she managed to laugh once again at herself. I told her it wasn't her, but that her computer was hard for me as well, and it was.

Eventually, I set it up for her so that she could download the chapters and find them with a click on a special icon. The first time she managed to find the chapter and print it out, Helene was quite proud of herself.

# HANDCRANKED CHAIRS
# FOR ALL

One day while biking with Helene on the boardwalk, she mentioned how she thought other people in the class might enjoy the handcrank. As she once said, "if it works for me, it should work for others." I was amazed at her attitude. Never letting her own problems get her down, she was always looking out to help others.

We talked about several of the more athletic people in the water class who probably would enjoy it. These were people who used to bike and participate in all kinds of sports before they contracted MS. Helene and I spoke to them. Most were hesitant at first, wondering if they would be able to do it. But as one lady said about Helene, "I guess you just don't say 'no' to this lady." One by one they began to try the chairs.

First, Helene arranged for some people to come to New York to join an Achilles club event and try the chairs. Helene stayed with them to teach them and give them the feel of the new equipment. Because it was difficult for most of them to come to the city, Helene brought the chairs out to them. She borrowed several chairs from the Achilles club and brought them to Long Beach.

One Sunday morning she took them to the boardwalk for anyone to try. Several people did and most liked them. Then Helene arranged for the chairs to be kept at the center where the water classes were held. Anyone with MS could use the chairs free of charge whenever they wanted. After each exercise class, Helene would encourage someone else to try a chair, even if it was just up and down the sidewalk or around the parking lot for a few minutes before going home. One Thursday when class was cancelled because the pool was closed, Helene had the class meet just to ride the chairs. I rode my bicycle, followed by several handcranks, with Helene as the tail. We made a caravan to the boardwalk where there were no cars to worry about. Helene coached them with the shifting and the turns; everyone enjoyed the activity.

Then Helene took off to do laps at her pace, saying, "I have a marathon to train for." As she sped away so quickly, one of the men looked at her disappearing in the distance and remarked, "that lady is not well."

I added, "No, she is not." Then everyone rode at their own pace, going up and down the boardwalk, waving to each other as they passed.

Whenever the pool was closed thereafter, the water class became a handcranked chair class. While the pool was being renovated, Helene turned the class into a land exercise class using the aerobic room and the gym machines.

She didn't want them to stop exercising, even for a week. "They can lose so much so fast if they stop exercising and I'm afraid if they don't come, they will get out of the habit and we may lose them."

This project was stopped by the MS Society that paid for use of the pool due to insurance purposes. One day, the main pool was closed and the therapy pool was too hot for most of the people with MS. People had shown up expecting to use the therapy pool or the gym machines. Rather than let them go home, Helene held class outside with everyone taking turns on the handcranks. Only one or two people from this class had tried the chairs before. Some were disappointed and were just going to go home, but Helene insisted, "You are here. Give it a try." And they did. They had great fun and a good workout, besides.

The most difficult part was getting the people on and

Learning to handcrank.

Helene, Jack Beanelieu (winner of the men's division) and Kyler at the Boston Marathon. May 2004. Helene had introduced Jack to the Handcranks.

off the chairs. Each one eventually found a way that was best for them. Some straddled the seat and lowered themselves in. Others sat sideways and lifted one leg over. But once in the chair, Helene would show them the brakes and explain the turns. In the beginning they didn't need to shift. Around the parking lot, then up and down the sidewalk and perhaps around the block. Then they were ready for the few blocks through the streets to the boardwalk.

One lady, very hesitant, said, "Let me try to get in it first." She sat in the chair inside the building, took one pedal and with a big smile on her face like a kid, exclaimed, "This is fun," as she took off through the lobby and drove it out the door.

Everyday it seemed someone else was ordering a handcranked chair and getting a workout they never would have gotten otherwise.

They told the others about how enjoyable and satisfactory it was to be able to "bike" again. Several entered an Achilles race as a team in a relay. One after the other, they began to buy their own chairs. As each one wanted one, Helene measured them and ordered it. She worked like a sales person. I told her she should get a commission from the company, but her only goal was to get as many people into it as possible to get the pleasure from it that she got.

It was exhilarating to see the smiles on their faces. One lady, who bought her own, now goes biking with her husband again. A few of them who would have spent afternoons at home were now meeting to go biking. It added something new and fun for them to do, and it was a great exercise as well. Helene had to prevent one man from buying his own handcrank, because his wife had called Helene, and said she wanted to buy it as a surprise for his birthday.

After a while though, problems arose. Tires would go flat, gears needed repairing and people wanted Helene to bring the chairs to the city to use in the Achilles races. Sometimes they would call her and ask for her to meet them so she could privately teach them how to use the chairs. Helene would agree.

One young man said hopefully, "I just want to be able to cross a finish line one time." A couple of weeks later after some training with Helene, he did.

Helene brought a pump to the center to repair the chairs, but it was getting to be too much. Helene confided in me, "I can't keep doing this," but it was more of a question than a statement. She seemed to feel guilty if she didn't. We thought of ways that perhaps instead of using them free, they could pay a small fee that would go to one of the gym's maintenance men and have him take care of them.

I reassured Helene, "You are doing way far more than your share. It is costing you money, and you are giving up too much of your time. Look what you have done for them already. Now you have to back off. It isn't fair to you."

With more of the people buying their own, use of the loaned chairs went down. Helene, except for placing orders, decided to put two of the women who were really into it in charge. They started a fundraiser to get money to buy the chairs, which cost from $1,200 to $1,500. They could work out some of the problems as to who would get which chair and teach others how to use them.

The chairs became more and more popular. Helene spoke to Robert Carroll, the recreation supervisor in Long Beach, and told him there would be handcranked chairs in the Memorial Day 10k run that year. Helene encouraged those with the chairs to enter the race. She recruited me to be the volunteer companion to bike along side as coach.

Two of the MS people finished the race and got their first athletic trophy in years.

One of the men, Darrol, had kept saying he didn't have the stamina to do it for a long distance. Helene and I both insisted he could build up to it. Helene would say to me, "We have to get Darrol into this." I agreed. He was the most athletic of the group and might have been a professional golfer if MS hadn't set in. With a bit of prodding from Helene and others, he got on the boardwalk a few times, but said it wasn't for him. With some more prodding from Helene, he reluctantly entered the Memorial Day race, but joyfully finished. Shortly after that, he ordered his own chair with special racing wheels, and got a racing outfit of helmet, jacket and shorts to match. I looked at the other smiling young man, and reminded him how a few weeks ago, he just wanted to cross a finish line.

"Now you did it," I congratulated him.

I kept praising Helene for all the pleasure she was bringing into the lives of others. Even people without MS, who for one reason or another couldn't bike anymore, were approaching Helene about the chairs. A new sport was catching on in Long Beach.

I turned to her and asked, "Just what are you going to do next?"

# KAYAKING

What she did next was to get people with MS to go kayaking with her.

A few years earlier, while Helene was still running, she took up kayaking. She got a two-man kayak and kept it at a place on the water in Island Park. "It was a great workout and a lot of fun."

She even got a wet suit to wear when she went kayaking during winter days. There are so many little waterways to explore off Long Beach. It is quiet and peaceful and you can get a lot closer to the wildlife with it than in a boat.

For George's 50th birthday they took a cruise to Alaska. Her son, Brian, was with them and for one of the side tours she went kayaking. Being "experienced," she signed up for the advanced route. They passed seals and exotic birds. They were told there might be whales around them, but not to worry. However, a single whale out by itself could be dangerous.

When they passed the seals, Brian remarked how cute they were. "No matter how cute they appear, they are wild animals and we can't get to close." Helene reminded Brian what the tour guide had said. Everything was fine and then all at once there was a single whale near the kayak. Brian was excited, but Helene was scared.

"He kept following us spouting and doing his thing, and I yelled to Brian to paddle harder." Brian is a strong young man and after a while the whale disappeared. They slowed down to once again enjoy the scenery, and the whale reappeared. It never bothered them and they returned to the boat with an adventure to relate.

Another time she invited Brian to go kayaking with

her and she would treat him to lunch. "He is strong and it is great to kayak with someone like that and I enjoy the time we spend together." Because she was with Brian, they decided to go to Jones Beach, a good distance from where the kayak was launched. It was fairly calm, so they went in the inlet hoping to see seals, but they had to fight the current coming back. When they finally got to the restaurant for lunch, tired and hungry, the place was closed.

"Let's try Freeport," suggested Helene. Freeport was another half-hour or so of kayaking and they were already pretty fatigued. Freeport is famous for its nautical mile of restaurants and gift shops, but today these were also closed. Now Brian was ready to kill her. Finally they tied up the kayak and Brian walked into town until he found a deli that was open and stocked up on food.

She took me out a few times. I thought I wouldn't be able to do it because of a shoulder injury. The first two times out, my shoulder pained, but no more than from other sports. The next time out, however, my shoulder was "cured." I don't know what happened, perhaps some scar tissue worked itself out, but that was the end to my shoulder problems. No more nagging aches. I could even throw a ball hard again.

"You cured my shoulder. Thank you!"

Helene protested, "That's not fair. My shoulder is getting worse." Helene had problems with her shoulder off and on for some time.

In our initial kayaking excursion I thought I should wear my wetsuit in case the kayak tipped. The water was still pretty cold. Helene assured me that the kayak wouldn't, indeed, couldn't tip. "I've had this kayak for six years, and it never tipped once, not even with my sense of balance."

Each cold day, I would question and she would assure, until I fully believed her, that the kayak could not tip over.

Again, as with the handcranks, we wondered whether some of the people in the class might enjoy kayaking. Jack was anxious to try it. He had kayaked before. Others were hesitant as they were with the handcranks. I told Helene I would go with her to help them get in and out of the kayaks. For the first time each one would go for short rides and then give someone else a turn. The kayak was for two, and very stable. Helene would be in the rear of the kayak at all times.

While we were planning this, Helene entered me in a short 3-mile kayak race with her. I wasn't sure I wanted to do this. "You are much more competitive than me," I said. "I don't want to train hard. I want to have fun. And if someone is ahead of us, and I have to kill myself to catch up, I would rather let them win. I'm not the one to race with."

Helene insisted that she only wanted to do the race with me. I acquiesced.

Even before this race materialized, Helene got the idea of a kayak trip around Manhattan.

"NO WAY!" I wasn't about to train for an 8-10 hour kayak trip, especially in the summer when I love the beach. I finally compromised, "Let's see how I feel after this 3-mile race coming up."

Before we could even practice for it though, Helene had the injury in the handcrank race, and with stitches in her face couldn't do anything. The day before the race, Helene got clearance from her doctor to do everything. She couldn't get a hold of me, which was fortunate for me. I wouldn't have been able to say no, and I certainly wasn't in shape to race. She found a strong man to be her partner. They raced and came in second.

Now she was focusing on the Manhattan trip. There would be one able bodied person in each kayak with a partner with a disability. It wasn't a race, just a fun trip.

The Achilles club had done this trip before. First, Helene had to get all interested to try the kayak.

One nice day she planned to meet Jack. "Let's see if we can get Darrol to do it also. He'll be great at it."

So she called Darrol and left a message on his machine and asked me to follow through.

"I really don't want to kayak," he explained. "I love the water, but I want to relax like on a nice sized boat cruising around, not working my arms off in a kayak. I get enough of that at the gym."

A little later in the conversation, "Maybe I'll come and watch for a while."

When I met Helene at the kayak, I told her Darrol was coming "to watch."

"How did you get him to come? That's great."

When Darrol arrived they talked a bit. He insisted, "I really don't want to do it."

Helene was standing on the sand under the dock. As he was saying this she reached up from underneath him and began to untie his shoes. She then came up, took his shoes off and put a life preserver on him, all the while he kept saying, "I don't want to do this,"

They went out for a short ride, and although he didn't admit it, we both think he enjoyed himself. Jack, on the other hand was super eager to try. He was waiting with newly bought bright colored water gear, and finished the 3-mile loop with Helene.

"It was easy. I just stopped to rest whenever I felt like it," he explained at the Monday night dinner. "It didn't matter, because I had an engine on the back," he laughed, glancing at Helene.

Helene began to focus on the trip around Manhattan. A couple of times she recruited me to go kayaking with people from the MS class that she thought would benefit from the trip and would also be able to do it. However,

Helene's MS began to affect her back and legs and for a while she needed a wheel chair. She ordered a walker with a seat so she could rest whenever necessary, and soon began to bounce back, although not quite the same as before. She and George took a cruise, and by the time she returned and felt well enough to kayak, there wasn't much practice time left.

Due to the September 11, 2001 attack on the World Trade Center, the trip was postponed, and Helene decided to give it a push again. We got two kayaks, Marie and me in one, and Helene and Marie's dad, Emile, in the other. Marie realized she would not be ready for the trip, but her father wanted to try it. Helene agreed to give him a "crash course" in kayaking.

They were to go out for a very long ride to see if he could handle it. I asked Helene how he did.

"We tipped over."

"What do you mean you tipped over? The kayak can't tip over. What happened?"

Luckily, they were not in the inlet where the current might have swept them out to sea. Helene explained that a big boat came by throwing an enormous wake. The kayak should not have tipped but as some water came over the top, Emile who was in the front and not used to kayaking, got scared and in a reflex reaction suddenly jerked to the side to get away from the wave. Emile was deaf and although they had hand signals for things such as paddle faster or slower, etc., Helene could not communicate with him as to how to handle the kayak through the wake.

"It happened so quickly. One second there was a splash, and the next second we were in the water."

Under ordinary circumstances, Helene would have been able to properly turn the kayak upright and climb back in, but her legs and back were still very weak. Also, Emile couldn't hear and he was a pretty heavy guy. Helene decided the best thing was to get to shore. She signaled for Emile to push the kayak to land.

"He is a strong man, so that was no problem." On the muddy marsh, Emile tried to get the water out of the kayak, but it was impossible to get it all out.

"This will have to do," Helene sighed, and they climbed back in, with their feet in the cold water, and clothes soaked. "That was a very long paddle back home."

On the day of the kayak trip, the weather was terrible. There were small craft warnings with rain and gale force winds predicted. I was sure the trip would be cancelled. It wasn't, and as long as the trip was on, Helene, the maniac, although not at her best, was game.

"Emile did quite well and made it to the last stop point. I was proud of him." Helene, on the other hand had kayak problems. The kayak took on too much water, and due to some defect unknown up to now as she never sailed in these kind of waters before, the water went to the front compartment and stayed there. Soon Helene, who was in the rear was up in the air. The rudder was too far up to steer, and they were forced to turn back. After an hour out, it took Helene two hours to get back in.

"I'm just glad you are all right", I said, relieved now that it was over." "I can't believe they allowed the trip in this weather."

I felt bad for her because I knew she really wanted to do this, but I couldn't help laugh at the image of her up in the air out of the water, trying to paddle.

The year before, there was a similar trip around Long Beach, but the leader wisely cancelled it because of the weather, which disappointed Helene. The following week, they tried again, but when they reached the inlet, he felt it was too dangerous and once again a disappointed Helene had to turn back.

"Maybe the fourth trip will go my way," Helene mused.

Helene in her first kayak.

# KYLER, THE INCREDIBLE DOG

Suddenly, the MS under control for so long, began to show its ugly head. Helene began to have bouts of nausea. Her back would hurt and she would have trouble moving. She started losing weight and had trouble getting around. Tests showed nothing wrong. She ordered a lightweight wheel chair and began using the walker with a seat on it. When she was tired, she could stop walking and actually sit on the walker. The doctor suggested a back brace, and one was ordered for her.

It was hard to see her like this. She still came to the pool classes, although she didn't go in the water as often as before, and taught the classes from the wheel chair or walker. It was especially upsetting for the people in the class. Besides feeling sympathetic and being very concerned, once again, it was scary to them. She was their role model and inspiration toward beating MS. If she couldn't do it, then how could they? Yet, through all this, Helene's spirits were always up and she was always pleasant to be around. "Life is too beautiful and precious a gift to waste on negative emotions. There are so many things I can still feel and enjoy each day."

One evening I asked Alan, who helped with the MS class, where Helene was. "Oh, she is still upstairs. She is exercising on the treadmill with her back brace."

The new brace allowed her to move again, so she started right in as soon as she got it. Some thought she was trying too hard, doing too much for her own good, but that is what made the "maniac" who she was, and where she is today.

"My legs were like mush from not exercising. I couldn't stand it, so I got moving as soon as I could."

During this time Helene got a call from Canines for Independence. A couple of years ago her doctor had suggested a service dog. Knowing how hard she was struggling for her independence, he thought it would be good for her. Helene put her name in, but was told there was a long waiting list. The timing couldn't have been better. Now is when she really had the need for one, more than ever. These dogs, like guide dogs for the blind, are professionally trained. They can pick up things, open doors, close doors and do a variety of miscellaneous activities to help a handicapped person stay independent.

Helene was very excited about this, and it boosted her spirits. She was sent a booklet to study which was overwhelming. "I'll never remember all these commands, especially with my memory. Some are different than what we are used to. Hurry means the dog is to go to the bathroom. I thought people use the term heel when they want the dog to walk right next to them, but here, heel means for the dog to sit by my left side. If the dog is on my right, and I say heel, he will switch to the other side of me and sit."

Then she added jokingly, "Maybe I can put a collar on you and practice."

I told her that I wasn't trained and would bite her leg. Then I reassured her by adding, "It's like learning a new language. It is impossible to remember everything at once, but as you use the commands over and over with the dog, they will become automatic."

For two weeks she was to attend all day training with the dogs, followed by a test and graduation. There were eight people there and about 16 dogs that just remained in one area until they were called upon. The people would work with different dogs and eventually one would be chosen for them. Cats walked all around, so these dogs would be familiar with them.

At first it was hard to get used to things. The first training was with the wheelchairs, and Helene said she was being pulled around all over the place totally out of control. When told to be firmer and clearer with the commands, Helene became louder and repeated herself. She yelled "SIT! SIT! SIT!" and every dog in the room stopped what they were doing and obeyed her command. They all sat at once.

With practice though, it became easier and she began to learn the commands. "These dogs are so amazing. We went to a mall where people were set up to come over with food and did other things to try to distract them, and we had to keep them on task. It seemed mean putting food under their nose, but this was all necessary so the owners could take their dogs everywhere,"

After a week, a dog, Kyler was given to Helene. Every dog from that litter had a name that started with a K. It was the same dog that she had picked out as being best for herself that the trainers also had selected as being best for Helene. They worked well together.

Helene said, "There was just something about him that separated him from the others." (I figured he must be the wildest dog there).

He is a beautiful big black dog that looks like a Labrador, but there is some golden retriever mixed in to prevent diseases of inbreeding. Because of this, there is a little wave in his coat.

Once the dog was chosen, Helene was to bring him home for the weekend. I immediately went to visit him. He sat still and offered his paw to me when Helene gave the command "shake," Sometimes he offered the left paw instead of the right, but other than that, this dog was like a soldier on duty. We went for a walk and he was perfect. He stayed right by Helene's side, and totally ignored passing dogs, bicycles, etc. Helene would say "no" as he looked at them, and then "good boy" as he followed instructions. He even leaned into her as she felt she was losing her balance, which gave Helene support to keep from falling.

When we got home, I asked, "Doesn't he get to play like a regular dog? It doesn't seem fair to the animal."

Helene said, "Oh, yes. Let's go out back".

We went outside into the yard, she said "release," and he ran around and around like any other dog would. It was like saying "dismissed" to a soldier.

I threw a ball, but when he brought it back, Helene told him to sit, and took the ball, and then he wouldn't run after it again. We realized that when she gave the command, he thought he was working again.

I said, "You will have to use a certain voice and commands with him when you want him to work, and another when you are playing, so he will understand the difference."

She again said "release," I threw the ball and this time when he came back with it, she didn't give any

Kyler

commands, just gave me the ball. I threw it again, and he chased it and was having a "ball" so to speak. He even began to dig up the yard, just like any young dog. In the house, Helene would say "lap," and this big 70-pounder would put most of his body on her lap and kiss her face, and love all the attention. He is just a big mush inside.

At the end of the second week there would be a written test and a practical one. Helene was nervous about passing it. If she didn't pass she wouldn't get the dog. This is good, because before the dog is given to its new owner, both the dog and owner are completely ready. Otherwise, it wouldn't be fair to the dog, and the person would not get the help needed from the dog.

By the time of the test, Helene was ready and passed. A graduation ceremony was held and she brought Kyler home. She was much more at ease with him than the weekend before.

The press and local news covered the graduation. Since Helene was well known, television did a segment on her. One of the newspapers included her picture. It was a decent photo of Helene on her handcrank on the boardwalk with Kyler next to her. The caption said "Helene Hines of Lido Beach takes advantage of a warm day with Kyler on the Long Beach boardwalk."

However, she wasn't mentioned in this article. Actually, the article was about mentally disabled people and had nothing to do with her or the service dogs, but there was her picture right in the middle of the article. So Helene got a bit of teasing about this.

That Monday she brought Kyler to the pool. Helene decided to sit with him and teach the class from there for the first week, rather than leave him alone while she was in the pool. I thought that was a good idea. By the second week, she had him stay at the far end by the office while she taught the class. Eventually, she would leave him there while she went in the water. After the session, he helped her pick up the equipment and put it away. With the back brace, bending over to get something was too difficult.

Helene brought Kyler to the after-class dinner. It was so amazing how well behaved he was at the restaurant. Everybody fell in love with him. It was hard not to pet him, but when he is working, you are supposed to leave him alone. The law states that a service dog has to be allowed everywhere, even restaurants, just like a seeing eye dog.

At home, Helene decided to do a laundry, something she hadn't done in years. As she dropped socks and shirts, Kyler picked them up for her. Helene seemed alright while she kept moving, but began having great difficulty getting up from a sitting position. She called Kyler over, gave the command to stand and stay, and leaned on him to stand up. Once she was up and moving she was fine. He just stayed by her side.

One day as I was getting out of the pool, Helene walked over with Kyler to talk to me. He looked at me with recognition in his eyes from the several times I had been at the house playing with him. I said to Helene, "I feel so mean ignoring him."

So she released him for a few minutes so we could say "hello." I think the release was more for me than for Kyler.

The next thing Helene wanted to teach him was to get the phone for her. "This way if I fall or something happens, I can say 'phone' and he can get it for me. I'll feel so much more secure." However, Kyler would mix up the phone with the remote for the television.

She decided to wait awhile before confusing him with any new things, until he and she were given more time to adjust.

Besides giving Helene more independence and freedom, Kyler provided wonderful emotional benefit as well. Although outwardly, Helene's spirits always seemed high, they really soared with Kyler, in spite of all the physical problems. "Kyler fills the world with love."

Physically, she improved as well. While the nausea was still there, it wasn't as bad. She began to eat better and put back some of the weight she had lost. She took Kyler with her to handcrank. During her bad days, she would not have been able to do this without him. And of course, she wanted to prepare for the next race.

As of this writing, the latest MS episode has subsided, and Helene is pretty much back to the way she was when I met her. The only difference is that where she goes, her faithful Kyler goes, too.

Her husband is still working as chief vascular surgeon, her son Brian is a chief uro-gynecologist, and her daughter Jennifer is an opera singer.

In April 2003, Helene was inducted into the Hall of Fame for Jewish Athletes. In January 2004 her shoulder had so deteriorated that she required a shoulder replacement. While still recovering from the complication of that operation, she entered the Boston Marathon and finished with one of her best times.

She has now taken up a new hobby – drawing with pastels. She is doing quite well with it.